Ethics for Educational Leaders

Weldon Beckner

Baylor University

PEARSON

Boston • New York • San Francisco
Mexico City • Montreal • Toronto • London • Madrid • Munich • Paris
Hong Kong • Singapore • Tokyo • Cape Town • Sydney

Vice President: *Paul A. Smith*
Senior Editor: *Arnis E. Burvikovs*
Editorial Assistant: *Christine Lyons*
Marketing Manager: *Tara Whorf*
Production Editor: *Won Jang*
Manufacturing Buyer: *Andrew Turso*
Cover Administrator: *Kristina Mose-Libon*
Electronic Composition: *Modern Graphics*

For related titles and support materials, visit our online catalog at www.ablongman.com.

Between the time Website information is gathered and then published, some sites may have closed. Also, the transcription of URLs can result in typographical errors. The publisher would appreciate notification where these occur so that they may be corrected in subsequent editions.

Library of Congress Cataloging-in-Publication Data

Beckner, Weldon.
   Ethics for educational leaders / Weldon Beckner.
     p. cm.
   Includes bibliographical references and index.
   ISBN 0-205-36091-2 (pbk.)
    1. Educational leadership—Moral and ethical aspects—United States. 2. School administrators—Professional ethics—United States. I. Title

LB1779.B43 2004
371.2'01—dc21

2002038641

Printed in the United States of America

10 9 8 7 6 5   07

Contents

Preface

About five years ago, I was asked to teach a course in the Baylor University "Scholars of Practice" doctoral program that would focus on ethics in educational leadership. The course had been listed in the program description for some time, but it had not been taught. I found the opportunity to be both challenging and daunting. Having little formal preparation or background in either philosophy or ethics, I was sure that those who had such training and experience would consider my entering their territory a bit unusual, to say the least. On the other hand, those with more background and experience in philosophy and ethics typically do not have much background in educational leadership. Putting the two fields of study and experience together in an organized fashion seemed to be a need in the area of educational leadership preparation, and little material was available. So I decided to "step where angels fear to tread."

This book has developed as I sought ways and means to teach the course in ethics for educational leaders over a period of five years. Students in the class have contributed to both the content and organization of the book; it is organized in much the same way as the class evolved. We have learned from each other, and they deserve much credit for the help this text may give to those who face the daily task of providing leadership for our schools and educational systems.

One of the most effective ways we have used to explore concepts and their application has been through the use of simple case studies from students' experiences. They were asked to write short descriptions of situations (dilemmas) from their experience that involved decisions with an ethical aspect (and we found that many, if not most, of the decisions required of educational leaders did, indeed, have ethical aspects). Several of their contributions have been included in this book, as is acknowledged where they appear. In addition, many of the questions and suggested activities accompanying the text material were suggested by individual students or brought up in class discussions. Unfortunately, it is not possible to acknowledge individual contributions of this type.

As stated in more detail in the introductory chapter, the book was written in an effort to help meet a perceived need to develop educational leaders who are more than efficient, leaders who effectively serve the educational and developmental needs of our children and youth. These leaders face in their daily responsibilities a multitude of demands and challenges requiring many kinds of decisions. Some of these are relatively easy to make, but many of them include what I have termed a "dilemma." No one very good solution or decision is available. Every option has one or more negative aspects. Making the best decisions in these kinds of situations involve more than following policies, rules, or accepted practices. Other considerations, typically involving ethical concepts, must be included in the decision-making process if the best interests of the students, the school, and society are to be well-served.

The basic purpose of this text is, therefore, to take what we can glean from the study of philosophy and ethics and find a way to apply the best thinking from these fields, and other related fields of study, to the everyday world of teaching, learning, and educational leadership. Scholars of these areas of learning may find inaccuracies or different interpretations of various concepts than they would normally use. My hope is that their criticisms will be muted as they recognize the limitations of expertise, time, and space under which a book of this type is written.

Our country and entire world need leaders who are willing and able to make difficult decisions in ways that serve the purposes of the organization and the larger society. This requires a level of ethical commitment and expertise that is often missing or neglected in the daily decisions of organizational leadership, be it in education or other fields of endeavor. Recent developments in the political and business world have made us acutely and painfully aware of this, and educational organizations experience similar challenges. Hopefully, this textbook will help prepare those who will be both willing and able to lead our world, through education, in the direction it needs to go.

Many individuals deserve recognition for their contributions to the development of this book. Parents, family members, teachers from the first grade through graduate school, colleagues, and students have all contributed in various ways. Special recognition is due colleagues at Baylor University for their contributions, often unrecognized, particularly Betty Jo Monk, Jimmy Williamson, Robert C. Cloud, and Chester Hastings. Jerome Stewart (school superintendent and former student) was gracious enough to read the manuscript and give valuable help with his expertise in ethics and philosophy. Research assistants Wang Ying, Sarah Bailey, and Lane Patton each made unique and valuable contributions to the effort. Many thanks to L. Nan Restine at the University of Alabama for her review of this text. As always, special recognition and appreciation are due my wife, Betty, for her support, patience, and skill in adjusting family matters and daily routines for the uncertain schedule and habits of a professor and writer.

Weldon Beckner

Dedicated to the teachers and educational leaders who work faithfully, often without due recognition, appreciation, or compensation, to make the world a better place for our children and future generations.

Introduction and Basic Concepts

1

Introduction

Sue is the assistant principal of an urban high school with a large number of minority students. One of her major responsibilities is administration and enforcement of district attendance policies. Juanita, the oldest of eight children in a single-parent family, is an excellent student (maintaining honor roll status) and well liked by teachers and other students, despite the fact that she is absent from school quite often. In fact, by mid-November, Juanita has already accumulated twenty absences, exceeding the maximum allowed for the year by school policy, which stipulates that a student may not miss more than 10 percent of the days a course is offered and receive credit for the course.

When called before the attendance committee, Juanita politely explains that her absences are due to a full-time job that she holds to help support her family. She further explains that her mother could not attend the meeting, as required by school policy when students are absent excessively, because of her work schedule. Juanita also shares with the committee her dreams of going to college to be a teacher, which is why she is working so hard to maintain her current grade point average.
(Contributed by Trae Kendrick)

Is the world "going to the dogs"? If so, are educational institutions contributing to this, and are educational administrators among the major ones to blame? Are they making poor decisions as daily activities and situations require judicious action? Judging from what you see (in person and on television), read, and hear, you might be likely to answer these questions in the affirmative. Although most of us do not agree totally with these kinds of charges, we would probably have to admit that they seem to have some validity.

Various areas of educational administrator responsibility could be identified as sources of the concerns expressed every day by the general public, writers, and commentators. These might include student achievement, the curriculum, student behavior and classroom management, teacher competence, and parental behavior, among other things, but they all have their origins in some basic philosophical and ethical questions.

Sue's dilemma may be somewhat unusual, but it illustrates the kinds of situations that educational administrators face every day. As they make the decisions required by their various responsibilities, educational leaders impact all parts of the educational system, particularly their own institutions, and most situations requiring action have moral and ethical overtones. Though most situations are not so complicated as Sue's dilemma, doing what one knows is right is not always easy, and even determining what is right is often difficult. Those situations that constitute a genuine dilemma (in which available decisions all have negative aspects or in which available decisions are equally desirable) are often the most difficult for educational administrators. What is the right and/or best thing to do? What can one do to be better prepared when it comes time to make difficult decisions?

To many educational administrators, philosophy and ethics seem rather far removed from the everyday challenges of educational leadership and management. It's a bit difficult to think about the "big questions" when the commodes are stopped up—or even when preparation for the next board meeting or a presentation to the Lions Club demands attention. However, some familiarity with enduring questions of humankind, how these questions relate to everyday challenges, and how those considered our best thinkers have dealt with them will help make the board meeting more productive and the Lions Club presentation more meaningful. Admittedly, getting the commodes unstopped may require less esoteric deliberation.

Administrators, including those who work in the field of education, tend to rely more on experience and personal judgment than on theory—particularly theories from philosophy and ethics. "Ready, fire, aim" is the pattern seen in many cases, so is it surprising that bad decisions are more common than they should be? Perhaps there may be little time for extensive consideration of alternatives, their probable consequences, or their ethical considerations. But it may well be true that enough time is available to make better decisions if adequate attention is given to basic principles of right and wrong and to guidelines for making difficult decisions and taking appropriate action when dilemmas occur or when right and wrong are less than obvious.

Perhaps we have been giving most of our attention to symptoms, rather than causes, as efforts have been made to improve education. How can a busy administrator know the difference? Are statistics showing increases in school dropouts the result of social circumstances, or might they be due to local disciplinary or promotion policies? Is cheating by students primarily a fault in student moral development or do teaching practices lead students to rationalize that cheating is a way to counter what they see as unfair in the system? It may be that educators and educational administrators are part of the problem as they follow misguided principles or practices with philosophical or ethical overtones. Perhaps questions and principles from philosophy and ethics will help those responsible for leading educational enterprises to make more ethical and thus more effective decisions addressed to treating the causes as well as the symptoms of social and educational ills.

Excessive attention to pupil testing, per-pupil expenditures, class size, discipline problems and policies, graduation requirements, and similar "objective" considerations as ways to evaluate and improve student learning seem to be examples of symptoms that are still getting most of our attention, rather than causes. Efficiency is often confused with effectiveness—efficiency in producing students who are able to quickly show on paper-and-pencil tests that they possess particular kinds of knowledge and skill, efficiency in developing the ability to win on the playing field, or efficiency in operating schools at the least cost. Educational leaders must be more than efficient; they must be effective in helping young people develop the ability to improve human well being in the face of increasing ecological and economic challenges around the world. This will require a higher level of moral and ethical thought than now exists among most educational leaders.

Purpose of This Book

I wrote this textbook because I believe that criteria beyond efficiency, or limited criteria for effectiveness, are needed in evaluating our schools, their teachers, and their administrators. Standards and habits guiding educational decision making must go beyond tradition, accepted practice, convenience, or intuition. Decisions must be guided by a framework of values that support what we believe to be the best for our society and our young people. This framework must be developed from a foundation of the best thought and standards available. Much of this framework is found in the broad field of philosophy, which we will not attempt to explore in detail. However, philosophy will be used as a springboard for considering the more specific field of ethics as a way to treat the causes of social challenges through educational leadership, because ethics and morality guide our actions and thus largely determine the results of our actions.

We need good leaders in education, professionals who show through example that they follow a system of personal and professional ethics consistent with the best social and personal convictions. But how should we decide what is best for our society and the individuals who make up that society? Again, it would seem appropriate to suggest that the study of philosophy and ethics may give good guidance in answering this and related questions. Stated in negative terms, Gardner (1990) has suggested that we do not need:

Leaders who inflict punishment on followers;
Leaders who treat subordinates well but encourage evil acts against others;
Leaders who use bigotry, hatred, revenge, or fear as motivation;
Leaders who make followers dependent; and Leaders who destroy human dignity (68).

The above statements and others we could readily add may seem obvious, but there is considerable evidence that our educational administrators do not always avoid these kinds of actions.

Unfortunately, there is no single set of ethical principles, no single set of moral concepts, upon which to base decision making in educational administration. As stated by noted ethicist Alasdair MacIntyre (1966), "Conceptual conflict is endemic in our situation because of the depth of our moral conflicts. Each of us therefore has to choose both with whom we wish to be morally bound and by what ends, rules, and virtues we wish to be guided" (268). Cultural diversity in our society results in conflicting systems of thought that claim to be guides for ethical action. Which claims deserve our allegiance? To answer this question intelligently we must study the major systems of thought and reach some conclusion about which ones to follow, or what combination seems best. Only then will educational administrators be able to give the kinds of leadership needed to develop good educational policy, assess the school's role as a moral agent, develop standards to govern the conduct of educators, and make the best decisions when confronted with everyday challenges and dilemmas.

In an earlier and more homogeneous society, desirable ethical decisions were easier to discern, if not always easy to follow. People tended to be directed by widely accepted rules and expectations. With the development of a more pluralistic society (and better recognition of that pluralism), more support for individual freedom, and more value given to the powers of reason, this relatively simple life has changed. The approach widely known as "postmodern" has encouraged "free" thinking and the loosening of the traditional ties that provided continuity and consistency, if not always justice, for our guidance in both private and professional settings. Now decision makers throughout our society must be prepared to apply more analytical and more relevant processes to decision making, especially in those cases where an obvious right-and-wrong situation does not exist.

There must be better recognition of the need to understand ethics and how to apply ethical concepts and principles to all kinds of situations. In an effort to help current and future educational leaders better deal with the above concerns, this book applies philosophical and ethical principles to the responsibilities and decisions required of educational administrators as they help mold the future through educational organizations and institutions.

Educational administrators will best approach basic philosophical and ethical questions by remembering that their central moral obligation is to serve the interests of students, and those of teachers, as they attempt to facilitate student maturation and learning. Acceptance of this principle seems to support the proposition put forth by Greenleaf (1977) that "the great leader is seen as servant first, and that simple fact is the key to his greatness" (7). This principle leads to a concept of authority "which holds that the only authority deserving one's allegiance is that which is freely and knowingly granted by the led to the leader in response to, and in proportion to, the clearly evident servant stature of the leader" (10). More attention will be given to this approach to leadership in Chapter 8 as an attempt is made to state guidelines for educational leaders to use in making necessary decisions, particularly those of an ethical nature.

Purposes of This Chapter

To help get us somewhat "on the same footing," the remainder of this chapter will attempt a generally acceptable definition of ethics followed by some typical ethical questions. This will lead into a more specific statement of objectives for the book and a brief historical preview of philosophy and ethics.

Definition of Ethics

Before exploring further the application of ethical thought to educational administration, some definitions are in order to avoid extensive misunderstanding and confusion. Most of us think we understand what is meant by terms such as morals and ethics, but closer examination reveals an unexpected complexity.

Aristotle, building on oral contributions of Socrates and those throughout pre-history whose deliberations and experiences influenced later thinkers, gave us early guidance about what came to be known as ethics. Aristotle's scientific tendencies may have somewhat inappropriately led him in an attempt to "make a science of what is in reality an art, the art of right living" (Hocking 1962, v), but that effort has proven valuable, if not totally adequate, to this day. He attempted to develop the standard of the "good." What makes an act right or wrong? "Is it the fulfillment of natural potentialities, the attainment of certain ends or results, or conformity with a formal or moral standard? Is there an absolute, universal standard of right and wrong, or are all such standards relative to a particular time and culture, or even to individual desires and preferences" (Hocking 1962, xv)?

The word *ethics* comes from the Greek word *ethos*, which originally meant the "accustomed place" or "abode" of animals. It was then applied to mankind to mean "habit," "disposition," or "character" (Adler and Cain 1962, 40). The related word *morality* comes from the Latin *moralis*, which pertained to customs or manners (Thiroux 1998, 3). The different concepts included in the two words are still important to our understanding of what is considered right and wrong.

It is not so important that we distinguish between ethics and morals, but it is important that we distinguish between morals and manners or customs. It is more a matter of custom or cultural practice as to whether a child should look an adult in the eyes when being reprimanded, for example, although it may become a moral matter if violating that custom becomes a breach of the ethical standard of respect for others and their practices.

Another area where custom is often confused with morality has to do with dress and "style," although style of dress may certainly become a moral issue if ethical principles are violated. One of the more difficult tasks of educational leaders then becomes that of distinguishing between what is moral or ethical and what is simply a matter of taste or custom. These kinds of determinations go a long way in assuring an appropriate decision and giving attention to causes rather than symptoms when differences in opinion occur relative to determining the "right" decision. Additional considerations may also be required, however, such as the political realities of the situation. Often a balance is required between the ideal and being able to accommodate political factors in such a way that one is able to "live to fight another day."

Aristotle saw the study of ethics as tied to the state of being "happy," or of the general well being of mankind, while recognizing the differences in opinion which occur. In his words, "All knowledge and every pursuit aims at some good. There is very general agreement . . . that it is happiness, and . . . living well and doing well [which is identified with] being happy, but with regard to what happiness is [both the general run of people and those of superior refinement] differ." However, after recognizing that people differ in their beliefs, Aristotle ventured to express what he evidently believed to be a general agreement that "the happy man lives well and does well; for we have practically defined happiness as a sort of good life and good action" (Aristotle, from Hutchins, ed. 1952, 340, 344).

Although there are many differences about the finer points, Aristotle's basic approach is still useful today. Serious disagreements may surface in attempts to define "happiness." Further differences are likely to present themselves as groups and individuals study ethics to promote human welfare, while facing questions about what is good and considering other words which present themselves, such as virtue, value, worth, principle, integrity, and (if the context is theological) righteousness.

Some Ethical Questions

In the study of ethics we encounter a variety of questions, some of which are general in nature and some of which apply more specifically to the work of educational administrators. They seek answers to the practical concerns of how to cope and how to make the best decisions in order to get through the day and help young people. Brief attention to some of these questions may help us better understand both the need for and the purposes of this text. They include the following:

1. What is the nature of morality, and why do we need it?
2. What is the good, and how shall I know it?
3. Are moral principles absolute, or are they simply relative to social groups or individual decision?
4. Is it in my interest to be moral?
5. What is the relationship between morality and religion?
6. What is the relationship between morality and law?
7. What is the relationship between morality and etiquette?
   (Pojman 2002, 18–19)

General questions such as those above lead to more specific ethical questions related to tension between individual concerns and purposes of the organization, fair compensation, working conditions, discrimination and affirmative action, and employee reward and punishment. In educational settings, questions related to administrator–teacher relations, student evaluation, curriculum and class requirements, dress codes, student behavior, honesty, student discipline, and teacher–student relations are typical of those encountered daily by administrators. Many of these questions pose dilemmas which have no completely satisfactory answer or they may more happily require a choice between two conflicting "goods." There is help available to the busy administrator facing these questions, but it requires a heightened consciousness gained through a deepened reflection and study of the society, the situation, and decision options.

Objectives of This Book

All of the discussion to this point leads to a more specific statement about the objectives of this book, which in turn may serve to guide both the writer and the reader. Our discussion has been basically one of description, description of need, definition, and ethical/moral questions that confront the educational administrator. The rest of the book will be more concerned with ethics as a way of thinking, telling us what to do or how to decide what to do. It will deal with philosophical and ethical concerns of leadership such as effect, motives, attitudes, beliefs, values, morals, will, commitment, preferences, norms, expectations, and responsibilities.

Throughout this book, emphasis will be on the practical uses of philosophy and ethics by educational leaders. As this principle is pursued, the following objectives will serve as a guide to content and organization.

1. To establish the importance of developing ethical educational organizations, leading to motivation for ethical decision making.

2. To show how philosophy and ethical theory contribute to ethical organizations and their leaders.
3. To develop awareness and sensitivity to what is ethically at stake in a situation.
4. To lay the groundwork for a theoretical framework from which the theory and practice of ethics in educational administration can be guided.
5. To develop skills of rational ethical analysis, identifying:
   a. The values in conflict in the case;
   b. The values which are most affected and most salient;
   c. The value actors;
   d. Intrapersonal and interpersonal distribution of the conflict;
   e. The hierarchical elements involved; and
   f. The basic issues involved (justice, equity, rights, etc.) and their application to the case.
6. To develop the ability to translate philosophical and ethical theory into practice.
7. To be aware of the need for and seek knowledge of:
   a. The task,
   b. The situation,
   c. The group,
   d. The individuals involved, and
   e. Oneself.
8. To help in the development of moral character.
9. To show relationships between ethics and religious beliefs.

Historical Preview

Before getting into discussion of the different ethical theories and how they may be applied to making decisions in educational settings, it will be helpful to take a quick look at how these theories developed and some of the important names associated with different historical and philosophical periods. Moral philosophy must be considered in relation to its history, because moral concepts change as social life changes and cultures evolve.

Early in the history of ethical deliberations we see basic differences developing which still prevail. **Plato** believed that moral concepts are intelligible only against the background of a social order. In attempting to identify the "good" in life, he concluded that it was directly related to one's station in life and to fulfilling the obligations of that station. In this way a social system could be developed that was good for everyone, as described in the *Republic*. Happiness was tied to the need for people to be virtuous, to live according to identified virtues. These virtues could be apprehended only by a few who had the necessary ability and training and then passed them on to others in the society and saw that they were accepted. These "virtues" will be discussed more later as they have been revisited in more modern times as guides for ethical living.

Other early Greek philosophers (the **Cynics** and **Cyrenaics**) disagreed with Plato and tried to develop a moral code that was independent of society and tied only to the individual's choices, thus attempting to make the individual moral life self-sufficient (MacIntyre 1966, 25). So we see Plato making ethics more relative to the society and others seeing it as independent of the changing culture and social situation. Does this sound familiar today?

Aristotle continued the work of his teacher and mentor, Plato, and attempted to develop a more exact and more usable ethic, still based on what is "good." He opens the book, traditionally known as the *Nicomachean Ethics*, with the sentence: "Every craft and every inquiry, and similarly every action and project, is thought to aim at some good; and for this reason the good has rightly been declared to be that at which all things aim" (MacIntyre 1966, 57). Either dedicated to or edited by Aristotle's son Nicomachus, the subject matter of the book is actually politics and the later work called *Politics* is presented as the sequel to the *Ethics*. As summarized by MacIntyre (1966), "Both are concerned with the practical science of human happiness in which we study what happiness is, what activities it consists in, and how to become happy. The *Ethics* shows us what form and style of life are necessary to happiness, the *Politics* what particular form of constitution, what set of institutions, are necessary to make this form of life possible and to safeguard it." Aristotle's word for *political*, however, "covers both what we mean by political and what we mean by social and does not discriminate between them." This was because in the small Greek city–state, the social and the political were closely intertwined (57).

Aristotle then gives a name to his possible supreme good. The Greek term he uses is usually translated "happiness," although it includes both the notion of behaving well and of faring well, reflecting the Greek idea that virtue and happiness cannot be entirely divorced. This "happiness" is achieved by being primarily engaged in an appropriate activity and by manifesting the "virtues" in all aspects of life (MacIntyre 1966, 59, 63). Just what constitutes these virtues will be discussed later. Restating the beginning sentence in the *Ethics*, to be considered good requires that it be something at which everyone aims, something which everyone considers desirable. This notion is moving in the direction of later statements by Kant, of which we will learn more shortly.

Building on the ideas of Plato and Aristotle, the later Greek view known as **Stoicism** developed notions about how to be virtuous and happy, ideas that had great influence on later thought. They greatly influenced the later development of religion and philosophy in our culture by describing how mankind may "attain inner control and peace" (Adler and Cain 1962, 71).

According to traditional Stoic doctrine, man is a microcosm corresponding to the macrocosm of the universe. Through reason he is able to discern the universal law and order present in nature and to live a life in accord with it. Through self-discipline and self-control he may attain virtue and happiness, which are mainly a matter of inner tranquility. Nothing else matters—external goods, common pleasures, even social ties.

> The world is providentially ordered, and any apparent suffering or evil is not what it seems but is part of a cosmic plan purposing ultimate good; apparent misfortune is only a divinely imposed trial and training in the attainment of virtue and indifference to external events. (Adler and Cain 1962, 74).

This kind of thinking may be seen in later theology and ethics of Christianity and most other major religions.

Greek ideas about the good life and virtuous living prevailed for several hundred years, the major change in western philosophical thinking occurring with the rise of Christianity. Christian thought, drawing heavily from earlier Judaic law, also contains some elements from Greek ideas, although Judeo-Christian doctrine emphasized the question of "What ought I to do if I am to do right?" This contrasted sharply with Aristotle's question, "What ought I to do if I am to fare well?" We are thus "moved from the well-defined simplicities of the morality of role fulfillment, where we judge a man as farmer, as king, as father, to the point at which evaluation has become detached, both in the vocabulary and practice, from roles, and we ask not what it is to be good at or for this or that role or skill, but just what it is to be 'a good man'; not what it is to do one's duty as clergyman or landowner, but as 'a man'. The notion of norms for man emerges as the natural sequel to this process, and opens new possibilities and new dangers" (MacIntyre 1966, 94–95).

Later Western religious thought brought a vision that went beyond that of Plato, Aristotle or the Stoics. Plato's vision of the eternal blessedness was that it is the reward of the righteous. Aristotle viewed contemplation as the divine activity through which man attains as perfect a happiness as is possible in the human condition. Epictetus, as typical of the Stoics, believed in a perfect contentment resulting from a willing conformity with nature and Divine Providence, based on an inner detachment from the body and the outside world (Adler and Cain 1962, 89).

Although there are numerous variations, the theme of Christianity, which strongly influenced Western thought, consists of three primary traditions, the first two of which evolved from earlier Judaic principles. These may be described as follows. (1) God is our father and commands us to obey his rules and moral principles. We should obey God because of his holiness, his goodness, and his power. (2) Even though God knows what is best for us, and it is therefore best for us to obey him, we fail to obey him and so become estranged. (3) We need to be reconciled with God, and this is done by affirming his sovereignty and accepting Jesus of Nazareth as his son and intermediary.

Based on the Ten Commandments and other early Hebrew teaching, Christianity has a strong flavor of universal rules, but it may be noted that Jesus' emphasis on "loving your neighbor as yourself" adds a dimension which requires determining what is best in a particular situation. Known by some as "situation ethics," a bit of relativity seems unavoidable as individuals determine how they would like to be treated in various settings and circumstances.

Thomas Aquinas put Christian ethics into a form which drew from Greek ethical thought in many ways but which was acceptable to church leaders. He proposed that the transcendental end of human activity, this being man's ultimate good, the final end of all human activity, is the God of the Bible, who was revealed to man in the history of the Jewish people and in the life and deeds of Jesus of Nazareth. Universal ethical questions are answered in terms of a particular religious faith, Christianity—a faith based not on the poetic myths or rational speculation of men but on truths believed to be handed down by God Himself through a special revelation. "Action and knowledge, hope, faith, and love are joined together in man's central urge toward his last end, his final good. In the grand view of Thomas Aquinas, the good for man is God" (Adler and Cain 1962, 90).

Aquinas accepted natural law as valid, defining a code to which we are inclined by nature. He added the supernatural law of revelation as complementing but not replacing natural law. Aquinas extended Aristotle's list of virtues, adding to the natural virtues the supernatural virtues of faith, hope, and charity. The nature of God was seen as the ultimate expression of the good, thereby adding a theological foundation to man's search for happiness.

Our next step in reviewing the development of modern philosophy and ethics is to consider the ideas of **Thomas Hobbes,** ideas that deviated significantly from those of Aquinas and other Christians. Hobbes believed that the developing world of scientific discovery could reduce the study of human affairs to reason, on the model of mathematics and the physical sciences. Based on considerations of human nature, he proposed that all individual judgments of "good" or "evil" are based on three types of endeavor. They are appetite (attraction to), aversion, and contempt (an attitude of indifference). These he believed to be relative to the state of a particular man and his body at a particular time.

According to Hobbes, the basic motivation of human behavior is self-preservation, which naturally results in conflict among people. Survival, or at least satisfying one's own desires, becomes the source of ethical behavior as people enter into a contract (which is understood but may or may not be written down) with a sovereign power to maintain peace and prosperity. Such a contract spells out what is and what is not just or ethical. "In the state of nature or war, 'good' and 'evil' are merely names for prior appetites and aversions. But in the state of civil society there is a common agreement upon what actions are rational and good" (Adler and Cain 1962, 121).

Even the Golden Rule, from Hobbes's viewpoint, might be interpreted as an expression of enlightened self-interest and expedience: 'Do good to others so that they will do good to you.' The virtues themselves are but "the means of peaceable, sociable, and comfortable living" (Adler and Cain 1962, 121). Natural law is reduced by Hobbes to self-preservation, which produces "appetites" (attractions) and "aversions," and no recognition is given to "supernatural law."

Accepting much of Hobbes's thinking, **John Locke** also gave prime attention to both our senses and to reason, proposing that we are born with a "blank slate" for a mind. He starts with the proposal that "our judgments of good and evil are merely expressions of the pleasure or pain caused in us by objects or the contemplation of objects. What pleases us we call good, what pains us we call evil. Pleasure and pain are also the sources of the passions—love, hate, desire, joy, sorrow, hope, fear, despair, anger, envy, etc.—which are simply 'modes of pleasure and pain resulting in our minds from various considerations of good and evil'" (Adler and Cain 1962, 191).

Locke suggested that there are three kinds of moral laws or rules: divine law, civil law, and the law of opinion. Divine law is known either by natural reason or by revelation and determines what our duties and sins are. Civil law is set up by political societies to determine guilt or innocence relative to civic matters. And the law of opinion measures virtue and vice according to the code and custom of a particular time, place, and society (Adler and Cain 1962, 192).

Locke recognized the unchanging nature of some laws, as determined by natural reason or divine revelation, such as the prohibition against murder. But he also accepted the position that reason and/or custom accomplished defining the type of killing that would be considered murder. Consistent with his "blank slate" theory, Locke proposed that our impressions of good and evil come as a result of both sensory and rational experience. One learns from experience what "killing" is, but to determine the morality of a certain kind of killing requires developing rational connections and conclusions, using intermediate principles and/or social practice as guides.

Locke maintained that mathematics could be used as a model to guide moral decisions, as particular actions could be deduced as either right or wrong by reflecting on the relationship of basic principles to specific actions. He suggested that ideas furnished by sensation about the world around us and what society (including religion) expects are connected by reason to produce concepts of what is right and what is wrong in a particular situation.

Martin Luther broke with many traditions of the Christian church of his time, particularly in that it was his belief that we do not have to depend on the church and its laws for guidance. We can have direct communication with God about these things as God reveals them to us through the Bible, prayer, and His Spirit. It was his belief that the divine commandments make up the only true moral rules and they require no rationale or justification, simply because they are the injunctions of God. "To obey such moral rules cannot be to satisfy our desires; for our desires are part of the total corruption of our nature, and thus there is a natural antagonism between what we want and what God commands us to perform" (MacIntyre 1966, 122). In direct opposition to Locke and others who would have us rely on reason for moral guidance, Luther maintained that "human reason and will cannot do what God commands because they are enslaved by sin; we therefore have to act against reason and against our natural will. But this we can do only by grace. We are saved not by works, for none of our works are in any way good. They are all the product of sinful desire" (MacIntyre 1966, 122).

Luther obviously moved far away from Aristotle, Hobbes, and Locke. "The true transformation of the individual is entirely internal; to be before God in fear and trembling as a justified sinner is what matters . . . not the action done or left undone, but the faith which moved the agent. Yet there are many actions which cannot be the fruit of faith; these include any attempt to change the powers that be in the social structure. The only freedom [Luther] demands is the freedom to preach the gospel; the events that matter all occur in the psychological transformation of the faithful individual. Good and right are defined in terms of what God commands" (MacIntyre 1966, 122–123). We are to obey God's commands because He is holy, all-powerful, and the ultimate definition of good.

Christian thought shares with Aristotle the view that we should not necessarily follow our human desires. But why should we obey current laws and customs—because God commands it? because they are prescribed by some sovereign or legitimate authority? because they will provide the most satisfying forms of human life? because we will be punished if we do not obey them? At this point Christianity makes a very important statement—that all men are equal in the sight of God. At the same time Christianity states that there are two kinds of moralities, moralities that are for a particular group and moralities that are for all of mankind. This is a particularly important contribution to morality and ethics, and it leads to a demand for at least a minimum of equal rights for all and a minimum of freedom for all (MacIntyre 1966, 147–149).

Traditional Christian theology proposes that there are universal laws and rules that all should follow, but different groups of Christians don't always agree on what those laws and rules should be. Different interpretations of Biblical instructions and acceptance of other sources of truth (such as personal revelations or mandates from church authorities) cause disagreements and confusion. Obvious examples from current controversies such as those having to do with abortion, the execution of criminals, or the "place" of women in society come quickly to mind. Additional attention will be given to the impact of Christianity on morals and ethics in Chapter 7. Later in this chapter the contributions of other major religions to ethical thinking will be briefly considered.

Niccolo Machiavelli deserves mention as probably the first after some of the Greek sophists to judge actions in terms of their consequences. To achieve the political ends he considered necessary, Machiavelli proposed that human behavior was predictable and that political ends could be achieved by following particular procedures and principles to influence the populace in general and individuals in particular to strengthen influence and maintain power. Machiavelli, supported by some medieval theologians, argued that certain political ends justified otherwise unacceptable means. In this way actions such as assassination of tyrants or maintaining of "natural frontiers" through military might could be "justified." The gaining and holding of power are argued to be the ultimate goals of social and political life, so as to promote order and prosperity. One may violate an agreement or break a promise if it is in one's best interests to do so, because humanity is at least somewhat corrupt and others will do the same. Generosity, clemency, and other "good" deeds have their place, because at times they, too, will serve the perpetrator's best interests.

The notion that actions may be judged according to their consequences will be found later in this discussion, as it was carried much further by Mill and his successors, although they weren't quite so "Machiavellian" in their ultimate purpose. The argument that "the ends justify the means" is basic for those who would allow the consequences of actions to be considered in making moral and ethical decisions.

Immanuel Kant, one of the true giants in the study of philosophy and ethics, will now be given some attention. For many, even those who have never given attention to philosophy, morality is roughly what Kant said it was. This may be because we tend to want a system of right and wrong, a way to make difficult ethical decisions that is relatively simple and unchanging. To many, black and white are more desirable than gray. Rules are much easier to follow in times requiring difficult decisions than are guidelines that require reason and analysis, and Kant gives us an approach which lends itself to developing rules which may be followed or enforced without much thought or deviation.

Kant sought a basic principle of morality, an unconditional ground of moral obligation that completely transcends the realm of sense experience and the specific characteristics of human nature. His aim was to construct an ethics completely abstracted from natural desires and ends, even from the generic human desire for happiness. He found the basis of such an ethics in the "good will," which wills only those actions that can, without contradiction, be made universal laws for everyone. Kant separated the essentially moral from what is merely self-serving, and he put the ground of morality in the will instead of in results. (Adler and Cain 1962, 207).

Developing what he called the "categorical imperative," Kant maintained that a rule or principle for right living must be universal, for all people at all times, in all places, and under all conditions. This contrasts with what he calls a "hypothetical" imperative, which is conditional on a want. According to Thomson (2000), the hypothetical imperative thus has the form: "If you want X then you ought to do Y," whereas the categorical imperative has the unconditional form: "You ought to do Y" (62–63).

According to Kant, to be moral, an act must be done because of a good will. Kant describes a good will as one that acts solely on the basis of duty to follow the categorical imperative. Things such as passion, self-satisfaction, the desire for happiness, or even benevolence do not provide its primary motivation. He believed that "an action is good not because it has good results, or because it is wise, but because it is done in obedience to this inner sense of duty, this moral law that does not come from our personal experience, but legislates imperiously. . . for all our behavior, past, present, and future" (Durant 1953, 209). Once it is established, one must proceed solely from a sense of moral obligation to follow a "categorical imperative," without regard for purpose, consequences, or personal feelings.

The "categorical imperative" concept is consistent with our feelings that some things are right and some things are wrong. Our actions, then, should follow those precepts that seem to be part of a universal law of nature. "We know, not by reasoning, but by vivid and immediate feelings, that we must avoid behavior which, if adopted by all men, would render social life impossible" (Durant 1953, 209). We may decide to lie to escape an immediate unpleasant situation, but we cannot be moral and will that lying should be a universal law. We know that to do so would create an intolerable world in which all people lied whenever it suited their best interests.

If Kant's notion of the "categorical imperative" seems to be a good one, then we could satisfy a desire to be moral by simply willing ourselves to obey such precepts. However, reaching agreement as to what those "categorical imperatives" should be is a considerable challenge, as indicated in the description of Sue's dilemma at the beginning of this chapter.

More recent reformers propose a return to a more rationalist, rather than an authoritarian, approach to determining morality, maintaining that in the end the individual must be sovereign. Contrary to Kant (as influenced by principles from Aquinas, Luther, and others), the emphasis turns to consequences of actions. Right and wrong, good and bad are to be determined by the attempt to produce the "greatest good (or happiness) for the greatest number." Basic moral sense is to be guided by the "social virtues" of benevolence and justice, aiming at the general good of mankind. Pleasure, then, becomes the ultimate end of human action, not pleasure in the hedonistic sense, but pleasure resulting from having done what is considered best under the circumstances.

Guided by ideas from **David Hume** and his principle of "utility," **John Stuart Mill, Jeremy Bentham,** and others developed the notion that mankind is governed by two things, pleasure and pain. Bentham goes on to define "utility" as that which "tends to produce benefit, advantage, pleasure, good or happiness (all of which amount to the same thing) either for the individual or for the human community. The good of the latter (of the greatest number) must be the determining criterion of the rightness or wrongness of conduct" (Adler and Cain 1962, 260). To determine what is the best course of action in a given situation, Mill and other "utilitarians" thus made a big circle back to Socrates, Plato, and Aristotle with the idea that competence to judge resides in the wise and good person who, through teaching and experience, has learned to make the best decision.

With Bentham and those who followed his line of thinking, ethics becomes very practical. Theoretical arguments are considered of little value unless they culminate in a better life for both individuals and the whole of humankind. He has little use for a system of ethics that allows suffering and unfairness to find acceptance within any system of morals, concluding that we must find ways to logically determine what actions will best benefit individuals and groups. In this way will the best system of ethics and morals be developed. Social and political reformers of his time and since then have leaned heavily on the ideas and logic of Bentham and those who then and now believe that the consequences of actions are more important than sticking to some law or rule that may produce unfairness and human suffering.

Charles Darwin supplied the basic theory behind the way of thinking about morality and ethics that we consider "modern." His theories about evolution are not limited to the physical development of natural forms. They also relate to how the moral sense develops, this being considered just as important to survival as biological evolution.

Contrary to what Darwin seems to have had in mind, the ethical doctrine that most social and political thinkers of his time drew from Darwin emphasized the struggle for existence and the survival of the fittest. When applied to people living in society, this became the right of the stronger (physically, mentally, socially, or economically) against the weaker. Evolutionary ethics then was used to justify unrestricted economic competition and "rugged individualism" in the extreme. Business monopolies, exploitation of workers, and cutthroat competition were justified with the argument that in the long run this would produce the strongest economic situation and best overall benefit for people in general, as well as those in control.

Darwin's theories are more likely to be used now to emphasize the elements of mutual aid, sympathy, and work of social institutions. This recognizes the fact that the social virtues are of mutually pragmatic value to all members of a group ("tribe"), becoming reinforced through habit, approbation, and blame so that they become social, rather than merely individual, patterns of behavior. Darwin thus maintains that the group with the most members possessing the social virtues will be the most likely to survive under "natural selection." The general "good" is supported as distinct from "happiness," which Darwin evidently associated with selfishness and personal pleasure (Adler and Cain 1962, 280–294).

This brief historical review would not be complete without mentioning the contributions of **John Dewey** to both philosophy and ethics, although he is best known as an educational theorist. Recognized as one of the most important moral philosophers of the twentieth century, Dewey connected "good" with action and stressed the need to avoid the tendency to abstract knowledge from both its sources and its uses. Knowledge is acquired because there are certain uses for it, so for him, "All reason is practical reason" (MacIntyre 1966, 253), and moral knowledge is to be applied to whatever purposes may be pursued.

For Dewey, "To characterize something as good is to say that it will provide us with satisfaction in our purposes." It will have practical benefits. To characterize something as "good" simply means that it will serve our purposes. In its extreme view, this leads to individuals giving attention only to their own purposes when debating right and wrong and ignoring the purposes of a larger group or all of humankind. Whether the action serves as a means or an end is not important. Means and ends should be considered together, as they are interrelated and complementary (MacIntyre 1966, 253).

Throughout this history of Western thought relative to morals and ethics, one may trace the influence of early and later **Judaic** concepts and beliefs. As discussed by Lawton (1996), the Torah expresses the commandments, which are "the headings for larger and more complex codes of legislation and guidance. The purpose of such laws is to define for the Jew the right and ideal life in relationship with his or her fellow human being and with God. The laws prohibit certain actions and command others, but in all except three cases are designed to enrich the individual's life." Indeed, "virtually every one of the rules can be broken if the purpose is to save life" (154).

Orthodox Jewish principles are described by Kasher (1989) as "first and foremost, normative . . . characterized by the rules that are followed, rather than with reference to preceding intentions, accompanying volitions, entertained beliefs, or achieved purposes" (130). It seems obvious that Kant and other similar Christian philosophers were strongly influenced by these principles, whether they knew it or not.

Modern Christian trends are similar in many respects to more liberal Jewish ethics. Shapiro (1989) states that a liberal Jewish ethic has at its heart, "You shall love your neighbor as yourself." This ethic "is not static but dynamic, and its dynamism has given birth to many denominations, philosophic trends, and movements, both religious and secular" (155–156).

Contributions from Non-Western Religious Thought

Our rapidly shrinking and changing nation and world and their increasingly multicultural nature require that we recognize the contributions of major religions other than Judaism and Christianity to modern philosophy and ethics, and this will be discussed more extensively in Chapter 7. Early Greek and Judeo-Christian foundations and traditions have obviously heavily influenced our thinking in the western world, but current regional and international developments make us increasingly aware of past and present influence from other sources, both religious and secular. Indeed, it is probably true that historical developments in religious and ethical thought in the western world were influenced more by principles from other religious and secular thinkers than was recognized then or fully understood today.

The more one studies and understands the moral and ethical principles embodied in the various religions of the world, both past and present, the more one must recognize the many similarities. Even a cursory understanding of moral and ethical thinking from major religions of the world today will help us to better understand, recognize, and benefit from what human beings through the ages have understood to be the guiding principles from religion for application to daily life.

Today's world is a place of contrasting dynamics and competing demands. As expressed by Crawford (1989), "Both the peril and the promise of world community have been brought about in our generation by the convergence of two forces of universality, one very old and one very new." An "old" force of universality may be traced to the religions and philosophies that displaced earlier tribal and imperial religions two to three thousand years ago. A "new" force is that of global interdependence, caused by revolutions in the fields of economics, communication, transportation, science, and technology (xi–xii).

If a global society is now evident, then it follows that ethics must be pluralistic. It becomes something changing and dynamic. It relies on a "common human nature" that "refers to certain properties, qualities, and energies that are universal, indestructible, and creatively expressed through personal styles" (Crawford 1989, xiv).

As we next consider in more detail the major ways that have been proposed to develop and apply a sense of ethics and moral behavior, references will continue to the historic milestones briefly presented in this introduction. Since I have leaned heavily on MacIntyre (1966) in this historical review, I will turn to him again to summarize the importance of historical moral developments:

> We live with the inheritance of not only one, but of a number of well-integrated moralities. Aristotelianism, primitive Christian simplicity, the puritan ethic, the aristocratic ethic of consumption, and the traditions of democracy and socialism have all left their mark upon our moral vocabulary. Within each of these moralities there is a proposed end or ends, a set of rules, a list of virtues. But the ends, the rules, the virtues, differ. For Aristotelianism, to sell all you have and give to the poor would be absurd and meanspirited; for primitive Christianity, the great-souled man is unlikely to pass through that eye of the needle which is the gateway to heaven. A conservative Catholicism would treat obedience to established authority as a virtue; a democratic socialism such as Marx's labels the same attitude servility and sees it as the worst of vices. For Puritanism, thrift is a major virtue, laziness a major vice; for the traditional aristocrat, thrift is a vice; and so on (266).

We will continue to ask some of the same questions the great thinkers of the past asked. Is an ethics based on uncertain estimates of consequences a satisfactory guide to human conduct? Or should we rely on an ethics based on fixed and absolute principles? Is some combination or variation of these approaches more realistic and practical? How will we best develop (for both personal and professional use) the best and most precise guide that may be used relative to particular ethical judgments and decisions?

Case Studies

A Teacher Becomes Ill

One of the best and most dedicated teachers in the middle school of which you are principal becomes very ill one day during school and has to be taken home. You then realize that this teacher has not looked well or shown her usual vitality lately. The next day her husband calls to say that she will need a few days to recover from an illness, so you obtain a substitute teacher. You learn through a mutual friend that the teacher has been hospitalized, and you call the husband to inquire about her situation.

The husband assures you that the teacher will be returning. However, he states that a few days will be needed for her recovery and that the teacher will return to work in two weeks. You learn from other sources that the illness was major, that the teacher underwent emergency surgery, and it was determined that she had inoperable brain cancer.

The teacher returns to work; however, she looks tired and frail. When you go to her room after school and ask about her health, the teacher admits that the doctors have diagnosed a brain tumor, but that it does not appear that surgery will be advisable, due to the location of the tumor. The long-term prognosis is not good, although she has been told that continuing to teach will not hasten the spread of the cancer. Indeed, the doctors advise her to continue to be as active as possible for as long as possible.

During the next few months, the teacher's vitality and effectiveness gradually decrease, and it begins to be obvious that student progress is being negatively affected. However, students do seem to be learning some valuable lessons about life, about helping those in need, and about cooperation as they assist the teacher with daily tasks and help each other with their lessons.

You discuss the situation with the teacher and suggest that she take disability leave, followed by early retirement. Becoming very emotional, she reiterates the advice of her doctors to remain as active as possible for as long as possible, stating that her continuing to work with her students is all that keeps her going. Teaching has been her life's work, and to force her to quit before it is absolutely necessary will make it increasingly difficult for her and her family to deal with her illness and probable early death.

Questions to Consider

1. As principal, what should you do to balance the needs of the teacher, her family, and her students, and to see that students get the best possible results from their school experiences?
2. Are there sources of information relative to this case that you should consult before making any decisions about it?
3. Are there additional options that you should consider, other than allowing the teacher to work full-time or not at all?

4. What school board policies or laws might apply to this situation?
5. Did you have the right to investigate the teacher's health, which might be considered a private matter?
6. If what is best for the teacher conflicts with what is best for the students, which should prevail? Why?

The Opportunity

Joe was ready and anxious to find a principalship. He had taught in public schools for ten years. During that time, he had distinguished himself as a classroom teacher, curriculum innovator, and campus leader. During the last three years, Joe had completed his master's degree and principal certification.

Joe was recommended by his university professors for a high school principalship, and the superintendent of the school district needing a principal asked Joe to come to interview with him and the school board. Although the school district was over 200 miles from his present home, Joe knew that the high school had a good reputation in academics and student activities. The school was not too big, nor was it too small. It was an ideal setting for a new principal to gain experience.

Joe knew that in two years the principal of his present high school (a truly outstanding and high-paying high school and community) was planning to retire. Joe's principal had already talked to Joe about taking his position when he retired, but he emphasized how important it was for Joe to obtain some experience at a smaller school. The principal, and Joe, too, felt that the superintendent, school board, and site-based management committee would have a much easier time accepting Joe as a principal if he had "proven" himself elsewhere. In fact, Joe's principal had already been talking with the superintendent and school board about bringing Joe back as principal after he had gained experience elsewhere. Everybody seemed to think that Joe's chances were very good to be named principal of his current school after gaining experience and showing his ability elsewhere.

Upon learning of his selection for an interview, Joe decided that he would call the superintendent. To his surprise, the superintendent invited Joe to come over for a visit. Joe left early one morning and planned to spend all day at the school. The superintendent and Joe hit it off immediately. It was as if they had known each other for years. Joe knew that this was the job he wanted.

As the day wore on, the superintendent called Joe into his office and shut the door. "Joe," he said, "I think that I can work well with you. The Board will listen to my recommendation. However, I cannot answer the questions the Board will ask you. I know that one of the major issues in the selection of a candidate will be whether they are considering this a long-term commitment or just a stepping stone. The Board wants somebody stable to come in here for the long haul. The other two candidates have both stated that they want to come into our community and make it their home. You need to think long and hard how you want to answer that question when it comes up. I can honestly say that someone who does not consider this a long-term commitment will have a slim chance of getting the job" (Contributed by Coy Holcomb).

Questions to Consider

1. If you were Joe, what personal and professional aspects of this case should you think about, and what answer would you give to the "big question" from the Board?
2. What ethical questions are raised by this case?
3. What principles of ethical conduct should guide Joe's thinking?
4. Is the saying "You should tell the truth, but you don't have to tell all the truth" ethical in this kind of situation?
5. Is it fair for the school board seeking a new principal to expect that the person employed commit to staying a long time?

Activities and Discussion Questions _____

1. Describe some specific moral/ethical conflicts that exist in our society today because of cultural diversity. Show how Aristotle's definition of happiness applies to your descriptions.

2. Pose some ethical questions that are important to you in addition to those listed in this chapter.

3. From the historical preview presented in this chapter, rate from one (extremely important) to five (not important) your opinion of the relative importance of the following people: Plato, Aristotle, the Stoics, Aquinas, Locke, Luther, Machiavelli, Kant, Mill/Bentham, Darwin, Dewey.

4. How would Darwin's ideas about "survival of the fittest" apply to ethics and morality?

5. Describe and give examples of the differences between ethics, morality, and manners.

6. Aristotle said "the happy man lives well and does well." Describe your current conception of what it means to "live well and do well."

7. Each person must play several different roles, both professionally and personally, in their daily life. Give some examples of how these differing roles may lead to "rules" or "virtues" which may conflict with each other. How do you reconcile these conflicts?

8. Describe the key principles that define your vision of good morals and ethics.

9. Why might the general public put blame on public schools and their administrators for perceived deficiencies in the world today?

10. Briefly describe a situation you have recently encountered in your work that illustrates an ethical dilemma.

References

Adler, M. and Cain, S. (1962). *Ethics: The study of moral values.* Chicago: Encyclopedia Britannica.

Aristotle. Nicomachean ethics. In R. M. Hutchins, ed. (1952). *The works of Aristotle, vol. II, Great books of the western world.* Chicago: Encyclopedia Britannica, Inc.

Crawford, S. C., ed. (1989). *World religions and global ethics.* New York: Paragon House.

Durant, W. (1953). *The story of philosophy.* New York: Simon and Schuster.

Gardner, J. W. (1990). *On leadership.* New York: Free Press.

Greenleaf, R. K. (1977). *Servant leadership.* New York: Paulist Press.

Hocking, W. E. (1962). Preface. In M. Adler and S. Cain, eds. *Ethics: The study of moral values. (v–x).* Chicago: Encyclopedia Britannica.

Kasher, A. (1989). Jewish ethics: An Orthodox view. In S. C. Crawford, ed. *World religions and global ethics* (129–154). New York: Paragon House.

Lawton, C. (1996). Judaism. In P. Morgan and C. Lawton, eds. *Ethical issues in six religious traditions* (135–174). Edinburg: Edinburgh University Press.

MacIntyre, Alasdair. (1966). *A short history of ethics.* New York: Macmillan.

Pojman, L. P. (2002). *Ethics, discovering right and wrong*, 5th ed. Belmont, CA: Wadsworth.

Shapiro, R. M. (1989). Blessing and curse: Toward a liberal Jewish ethic. In S. C. Crawford, ed. *World religions and global ethics* (155–187). New York: Paragon House.

Thiroux, J. (1998). *Ethics: Theory and practice, 6th ed.* Upper Saddle River, NJ: Prentice Hall.

Thomson, G. (2000). *On Kant.* Belmont, CA: Wadsworth/Thomson Learning.

2

Philosophical Concepts Important to the Study of Ethics

Eleanor has been informed by a school board member that one of her assistant principals is having an affair with one of the teachers in the middle school of which she is principal, although to her knowledge no indiscretions have occurred on campus. Both the assistant principal and the teacher are married, with small children. She overheard several students joking about the affair in the cafeteria during lunch. Parents are beginning to talk and teachers are concerned about the impact on student morals and community support. (Contributed by Lee Stewart)

Ethics is a study of ideas, ideas about right and wrong, and these ideas are couched in terms and concepts which require definition and understanding. Before getting into the general consideration of how educational administrators may better follow ethical principles, we must reach some personal and professional conclusions about the meaning and issues surrounding concepts important to that study. This could include a long list of terms, but our focus will be limited to a few of the most prominent. Others will be included in the context of later discussions.

Many of the terms and concepts related to ethical discussions have direct connections to each other. So, although the following discussion will be grouped according to particular words, we must recognize that there are connections and take them into consideration as issues related to the various concepts are considered. For example, the concept of rights is directly related to ideas about freedom, as well as the other topics that follow. To some extent, they must be considered as a whole, rather than as discrete words to define and apply.

Rights

Americans and others with a democratic heritage tend to be strong believers in "rights." But what constitutes a right? Consider the following:

Does a teacher have the right to "moonlight" twenty or thirty hours per week?

Does a teacher have the right to smoke, though a student may not?

Does a parent have the right to know how a student's grade was determined?

Does a teacher have the right to an extramarital affair? Or to live with a person of the same sex?

Does a teacher have a right to teach past the age of "normal" retirement?

Does a teacher have the right to decide how student grades should be determined?

Does a student (or parent) have the right to see all of the student's personal school records?

Does a principal have the right to decide who should be employed as a teacher at his/her school?

Does a principal have the right to decide how teachers should dress at school?

Does a student have the right to decide what his/her hair color will be?

Does a student have the right to decide where to sit in a classroom?

Does a student have the right to bring articles of self-defense to school?

Educators have a responsibility to respect the rights of others, both as a moral duty and as role models, but disagreement occurs about what rights should apply in a given situation or what constitutes violation of a person's rights. In addition, we must recognize the fact that every right that one person has places a responsibility on someone else. How, then, may we define and describe what is meant by "rights"? What are the origins of human rights and what areas of application may serve to exemplify the complexity of issues and arguments concerning rights?

Definition and Descriptions.   We tend to think of rights as something inherent and unquestionable. This seems to imply that rights are the same for everyone and in all situations. According to Ottensmeyer and McCarthy (1996), "When we say that a person has a moral (or legal) right in a given situation, we mean that it is ethically (or legally) permissible for him or her either to act in a certain way or to insist that he or she be treated in a certain way without obtaining anyone's permission to do so" (15). If this is true, does it mean that a person's rights cannot be limited in certain situations? And who is responsible for seeing that my rights are granted or enforced? What rights do I have to forcefully protect my rights? These and other questions about rights make the daily news or may come to mind relative to daily life and circumstances.

Some rights may be recognized as **absolute,** in that they prevail in all circumstances. Our forefathers considered "life, liberty, and the pursuit of happiness" to be inherent rights in most circumstances, but these are overridden or forfeited at times, according to modern law and practice.

Most rights are ***prima-facie,*** they may be overridden if justified by circumstances. But how do we decide what circumstances should result in limiting or forfeiture of a person's rights? Are there rules for this? Dilemmas occur, for example, when administrators must decide when a *prima-facie* right, such as the right to personal preference in dress style or freedom of speech in the classroom, should be overridden.

Some rights are positive, others are negative. A **negative right** is a right to be left alone, to not interfere with what one wants to do. A teacher's personal lifestyle outside the school setting or right to earn extra income after school hours might be argued to be negative rights. The major "freedoms" spelled out in the Constitution and Bill of Rights are basically negative rights, although there may be times when positive action must be taken to protect those freedoms.

A **positive right** requires others to assist in its exercise, usually through some governmental entity. Rights to "equal opportunity" through affirmative action may require preferential treatment for those whose socioeconomic situation is unfortunate or whose past social circumstances have been unfair and adversely affected their ability to achieve certain privileges. Equal opportunity for all young people to receive a good education may require the transfer of tax revenues from one school district to another. The right of those challenged physically or mentally to have equal opportunities in education and in life has brought about massive changes and adaptations in our educational system and in other areas of public and private life. Positive rights tend to be much more controversial than negative rights, although many times more heat than light has been generated around both.

Rights may also be classified as either general or particular. **General (or human) rights** are obtained simply by being human. Negative human rights include life, physical property, due process, privacy, autonomy, freedom of thought and expression, and private ownership of property. Positive human rights are generally thought to include food, adequate housing, competent medical care, employment at a living wage, and education, although as mentioned above, there tends to be more disagreement about positive rights.

Particular rights depend on specific circumstances. For example, a person who is promised something usually has the right to receive it. Some particular rights are role-based, such as those concerned with relationships between parents and children, professionals and clients, employers and employees, and students and teachers. Parents have rights relative to their children that others don't have, such as determining methods of discipline or making decisions about their education. Medical and legal professionals have rights relative to maintenance of privacy concerning their clients, and employers have rights to determine working conditions, wages, and productivity requirements of their employees. All of these rights are tempered by responsibility, the rights of others, and what is considered appropriate in each situation as determined by various kinds of interlocking rights and responsibilities (Ottensmeyer and McCarthy 1996, 15–16).

Sources of Rights.   As stated by Barrow (1975), "when we appeal to rights we are appealing to a presupposed moral schema or set of rules. We assume and implicitly demand that others share our assumptions, that there is a particular system of moral rules binding on persons, such that it is true that a person ought to be free, ought to be self-governing, ought to be educated and so on" (143). The source and authority for establishing rights which are to be respected and maintained by a group or a society have been argued since the beginning of philosophical and ethical thought.

Human rights have usually been argued as originating either from **natural law** or **divine law.** Rights argued according to these alleged sources may be similar, but they may differ considerably. Dangers are evident in each argument. Natural law may be used as rationale to support a particular bias, such as privileged status determined by sexuality, intelligence, economic status, social class, or race.

Divine law, because it is supposedly created at a supernatural level, may be considered beyond question or argument, making it very difficult to bring about needed social or economic change. And, of course, divine law is subject to development or interpretation by those who have managed in some fashion to achieve the status of divine oracles. What was once custom or cultural preference may over time achieve the status of divine law and give unwarranted strength to tradition or some written record that is considered divinely created or inspired. An even greater danger is that those who have achieved a high level of authority or acceptance in a particular religious group may be able to interpret and mold divine law to suit their own biases and purposes. Again, everyday practices relative to dress style or what more properly should be considered "manners" may be maintained with arguments related to divine law.

Natural law rights, explains MacIntyre (1966), are those argued on the basis that they exist simply because we are human. They form "the means to the most satisfying forms of human life" (147). "The doctrine of natural rights, (founded on concepts of natural law) claimed that no one has a right against me unless he can cite some contract, my consent to it, and his performance of his obligations under it" (155).

Using Darwin as their authority, some argue that natural laws resulting in the "survival of the fittest" should be followed for the ultimate benefit of humanity. This argument supports rather extreme concepts of freedom and liberty as natural laws. A contrasting approach (also citing Darwinian authority) argues the need for mutual aid as the natural means of survival.

Divine law in the Christian tradition exists because God authorizes it. All men and women are considered equal under the tenets of divine law, which are spelled out in scripture or the mandates of religious authority. This authority also legitimizes the authority of superiors and temporal rulers. Our natural desires are not taken as necessarily acceptable (MacIntyre 1966, 149, 155).

Concepts and arguments about rights are tied closely to notions of equity, justice, and freedom, which are discussed more fully below. These exemplify some of the strongest and most universally held beliefs about rights. Few would argue against equity, justice, and freedom, but there is considerable disagreement about their definition and application.

Areas of Application.   It isn't difficult to identify examples of disagreement in applying concepts and beliefs about rights. Notions about employee rights and privacy relate to the status of women on the job, employer sanctions that limit speech, "whistle blowing" and professional responsibility, and employee security. What legitimate rights do employees have when they enter the workplace, and under what, if any, conditions can these rights be overridden by an employer?

The concept of affirmative action raises many areas of disagreement about rights. There are at least three current positions on this subject: (1) opposition to any consideration of race or gender in the decision-making process; (2) support for broadening equality of opportunity without lowering standards for qualification; and (3) use of preferences, such as quotas, timetables, and reevaluation and lowering of qualifications to achieve goals.

Gender equity questions include "comparable worth" arguments for determining wages and benefits, equal opportunity for employment and promotions, and arguments based on different roles for women in home and society. Should "equal pay for equal work" rights include "equal pay for comparable work"?

Many related questions come quickly to mind. For example, should salaries give primary attention to "merit"? If so, how is merit determined and measured? Does fairness imply salary and benefits based on seniority? If not, how should these be determined?

What is the appropriate relationship of an individual's personal rights and those of others? For example, does my right to bear arms supercede the safety rights of others? Do my freedom of speech rights supercede the religious or moral preferences of others? Do my rights to privacy carry more weight than "the public right to know"?

Do employers have the right to pay salaries and provide working conditions as they see fit for the benefit of the business? Is employment a right or a privilege? When may contractual agreements be legitimately broken? Do employees have the right (or even the obligation) to report illegal or perceived improper actions of their employer? If so, to what extent should this right be protected?

Conflicts between autonomy and authority provide many difficult situations regarding rights. Do teachers have the right to determine how they will conduct their classes or does the principal have the right to monitor and control teacher actions? Is "academic freedom" a legitimate concept? If so, how should it be protected or controlled? Should students have the autonomy to decide how they will dress or decorate their bodies for school or should school authorities be able to modify this right, and to what extent? Should local school officials have the right to decide if public prayer at high school football games is allowed, or should state or federal authority make this decision? These and many similar ethical questions come out of our concern for rights.

Freedom

The concept of *freedom* is related closely to that of rights and dear to the hearts of Americans, along with the related notions of liberty, independence and individuality. Our history books are full of praise for the desire that our forefathers showed to escape economic and/or religious bondage in a new land of freedom and opportunity. As noted by Ladd (1995),

> many analysts from Alexis de Tocqueville on down to the present have observed [that] the core of the sociopolitical ideology on which the U.S. was founded is a uniquely insistent and far-reaching individualism—a view of the individual person which gives unprecedented weight to his or her choices, interests, and claims. This distinctive individualism has always enriched the moral life of the country in important regards and posed serious challenges to it in yet others (236).

But we also recognize the limits to freedom. In the vernacular, "your freedom ends where my nose begins." Establishing the appropriate and acceptable limits to this freedom becomes a source of considerable disagreement. Critics of the "dark side" of individualism charge that it has come to emphasize the gratification of the self over the needs of important social institutions, such as the family. They note that the natural tendencies of individualism toward narrow self-service have historically been mitigated by religion and local community ties, but radical insistence upon individual autonomy has been to the detriment of the family and other collective institutions that depend on substantial subordination of individual claims.

The extremes of the above tendency may be observed among those known politically as "libertarians." They do not advocate always maximizing liberty, because it is generally not supported that one person's liberty should be violated to increase the liberty of others. But, according to Harwood (1993), the definition of libertarianism does include the following principles.

1. Anything between consenting adults is morally permissible.
2. *Laissez-faire* capitalism is morally required. This includes *caveat emptor* (let the buyer beware) rather than government safety or health regulations.
3. Coercion (the deprivation of liberty) is wrong except to punish criminals, to defend against an immoral attack, and to supervise the mentally incompetent (e.g., children, the senile, the retarded, and the insane).
4. Promises must be kept, and fraud is wrong.
5. Government should be minimal; it should be as a night watchperson limited to peacekeeping functions (the police and the military) enforcing principles 1–4 above with as little force as possible (24).

Others have presented views consistent with what we would consider to be a more generally accepted position. As noted by MacIntyre (1966), the prominent nineteenth century philosopher John Stuart Mill, for example,

> argued eloquently in favor of the principle that "the only purpose for which power can be rightfully exercised over any member of a civilized community against his will is to prevent harm to others" and that "The only part of the conduct of any one for which he is amenable to society is that which concerns others."
>
> The general conclusion to be stressed . . . is that we need not a supposedly self-evident principle of non-interference, but principles of legitimate interference, rules which distinguish acceptable from unacceptable ways of affecting other people—perhaps quite radically—where the acceptable ways are those that in the concrete situation harmonize with the general form of conditions for the good life.
>
> Liberties conflict with one another, and almost any policy whatever can be represented as a defense—direct or indirect—of some sort of liberty. What we need, therefore, is not a general defense of liberty, but adjudication between particular rival claims to freedom. For example, parents claim the freedom to bring up their children as they see fit, but this

may interfere with the freedom of the children to develop their own opinions and views.

Even those with beliefs at the opposite end of the spectrum in many ways from those of the Libertarians argue their case in terms of freedom. Marx, for example, sees freedom as overcoming the limitations and constraints of one social order by bringing another, less limited social order into being. According to him, a socialist society frees a person from constraints imposed by capitalism and the ruling class which limit his freedom ". . . in a set of relationships which nullify his civil and legal freedom and stunt his growth" (180–182, 212).

As with the concept of rights, the concept of freedom requires balance and limitation. The search for Aristotle's "golden mean" again becomes attractive, but the location of this "golden mean" relative to the various "freedoms" we value becomes a matter of considerable disagreement and controversy.

Responsibility

Rights and freedom, of course, carry *responsibility*—responsibility for the consequences of the actions that may result from exercising various rights and freedoms. Some of these consequences are obvious and it is not difficult to decide if they are right or wrong. Exercising my rights at the expense of someone else's rights is generally recognized as wrong. However, are there times when this would be appropriate? In school settings, for instance, there are often times when a school administrator must restrict the right of a student to act in a way which would be harmful to or restrict the rights of other students. Other examples of dilemmas faced by school administrators relative to the rights of others include those instances when parents may want to exercise their freedom to take their child out of school for an extended period of time to attend the distant funeral of a deceased relative. To restrict these desires may be contrary to the culture of the family and, in some ways, contrary to the best interests of the child. But, at the same time, there is a responsibility for the educational welfare of the child that both the parents and school authorities must consider.

Responsibilities are both positive and negative. Some philosophers have argued that a person is responsible only for those actions taken in a purposeful fashion, that one is not responsible for not taking action. Others argue that one is responsible both for actions taken and those not taken. The classic example of this question involves a trolley driver who is suddenly aware that five workers are in the path of the trolley and he cannot stop in time to avoid hitting them. However, he can turn off on a side track where only one person (a little girl playing with her doll) would be in the path of the trolley. Some would say the driver would not be responsible for the deaths of those in the direct path of the trolley because they will be killed if he does nothing, while he would be responsible for the one person on the side track if he turned onto it, because he would be taking positive action to avoid the five if the one is killed. Others would argue that responsibility lies in diminishing evil by taking action to avoid hitting the five, even if the action results in the death of the one.

Most of us would argue the validity of being responsible for both action and failure to act. However, the matter becomes complicated when degrees of misfortune are in question, such as whether to spend very large sums of money to meet the needs of one exceptionally handicapped student or to allow that money to be used for the benefit of the general student population and neglect the needs of the handicapped student. Other questions of responsibility face teachers and administrators every day, such as whether they are responsible for seeing that students succeed or just for giving students the opportunity to succeed.

Employee responsibility is usually thought to include loyalty to the organization and to fellow employees (teachers and administrators). On the other hand, responsibility may include the moral obligation to report wrong-doing by peers or certain employees of the organization. Administrators are expected to be loyal to (and "support") their teachers. But what if the teacher is not fulfilling some of their professional responsibilities, "stretching the boundaries" of acceptable moral behavior, or being overly strict with students? Another right, that of social interaction, may become sexual harassment if "behavior . . . seeks sexual ends without any concern for the person from whom those ends are sought, and which typically produces an unwanted and unpleasant response in the person who is the object of the behavior" (Scott and Wong 1996, 371).

Is a person responsible for their actions when carrying out the orders of superiors? What should be done if those orders are considered immoral or unethical? Who is to judge?

So we again see how educational leaders may face dilemmas requiring ethical decisions, this time in the highly valued areas of freedom and responsibility, when action consistent with one concept will result in neglecting or ignoring the other. Confronting these kinds of conflicting responsibilities is one of the most common ways that educational leaders experience ethical dilemmas, being caught between incompatible alternatives or being torn between two sets of expectations or inclinations, neither of which is without significant costs.

What to do? As pointed out by Barnard (1964), if the situation is not handled wisely, such conflicts may result in several possible consequences.

1. General moral deterioration as manifested in frustration and inability to make decisions.
2. A diminution of the sense of responsibility demonstrated by a tendency to allow incidental or external pressures and chance determinants to make decisions for us.
3. Withdrawal from active involvement in the arena of decision making, such as resignation, a leave of absence, or retirement.
4. Development of an ability to avoid responsibility by steering clear of conflict situations that may require difficult decisions.

5. Development of the ability to construct alternative measures that satisfy immediate desires or requirements without violating any codes (271–272).

Obviously the desirable result is the last, but being able to produce it requires considerable knowledge, skill, and good judgment.

Duty

The concept of *duty* is another source of difficulty in leadership ethics because conflicting duties may exist in the same situation. Duty and responsibility are sometimes considered synonymous, but those who stress the overriding importance of duty are more prone to emphasize following the demands of a duty to the detriment of other values. Among school administrators this is often evident in the tendency to dutifully enforce rules which are obviously unfair or unwise in certain situations.

As explained by Pojman (2002), to be considered a moral person by those who emphasize the concept of duty, "one must perform moral duty solely for its own sake ('duty for duty's sake')" (142). One must tell the truth because it is the right thing to do, not just because it will be more likely to keep you out of trouble. In the moral system of Kant (discussed later in this book), all duties fall into the language of imperatives or commands. **Hypothetical imperatives** (do one thing to achieve another) are not the kind of imperatives that characterize moral actions. To Kant, this is getting too close to what we might today call "situation ethics." Kant prefers what he calls **categorical imperatives.** Simply say "do this," and these imperatives form the rules for moral action. In Chapter 3 we will investigate how one may identify so-called categorical imperatives. Moving on into Chapters 4 and 5, we will see how ethical theories are either duty-oriented, action-oriented, or motive-oriented.

Philosophers who disagree with the unyielding absolutism of Kant's theories take the position "that we have certain *prima facie* duties that we must always adhere to *unless* serious circumstances or reasons tell us to do otherwise. As suggested by Ross (1930) this approach suggests that "consequences [do not] make an action right or wrong, but . . . it is necessary to consider consequences when we are making our moral choices" (65).

One of the more common situations where different "duties" collide happens when an employee has knowledge of wrongdoing by superiors or colleagues. Such an employee is confronted with the dilemma of making a choice between loyalty to one's employer, superior, or colleague and the duty to "blow the whistle" and report to the proper authorities what is considered wrongdoing.

When is "whistle blowing" appropriate and wise, particularly if it involves the action of a superior in the organization? It may be internal, occurring when a member of an organization reports suspected wrongdoing within the organization, either through the customary chain of command or outside the chain of

command. Or it may be external, when the whistle blower reports his or her ob-
servations and assessments to someone outside the organization.

Those who criticize whistle blowers maintain that they have a duty to be
a member of a team—to be loyal. They are expected to exercise a formal duty
to the organization and an informal duty to colleagues, duties that are considered neglected if a person becomes an "informer." However, as explained by
Ottensmeyer and McCarthy (1996), "in their roles as employees or managers
people do have a legal and ethical duty of loyalty to the organization for which
and in which they work; they have an obligation to promote the best interests
of those firms and businesses that pay their salaries. What the critics fail to see,
however, is that these ethical duties, though real, are *prima facie*, that is, . . .
they can be overridden by other, more ethically pressing, obligations and duties" (418). Loyalties may appear at first glance to be an obligation, but
upon further examination or presentation of further evidence (in the legal
field), one may judge that they should be less important than other considerations.

In the field of education, the question often becomes one of loyalty to the
organization, one's colleague, or a subordinate (which perhaps should be considered a *prima facie* duty) versus loyalty to the needs of children or some more
universal standard. For example, should marginally effective teachers continue
to be employed because they need the income and have children who are de-
pendents, or should termination be pursued in the interests of those teachers'
students? If a teacher has knowledge of a superintendent's misuse of small
amounts of school funds, should that teacher report the misuse to a school
board member? Would it make any difference whether the superintendent
was very good (successful in providing very good opportunities for students),
average, or less than competent? At what point should loyalty to one's
colleagues, students, and/or the organization be overridden by the duty to protect the welfare of children or maintain honesty among teachers and administrators?

Ross (1930) identifies a *prima facie* duty (one that may be overridden in
certain circumstances) as "one that all human beings must obey in a general way
before any other considerations enter into the picture" (Thiroux 1998, 65).
Some of Ross's *prima facie* duties are:

1. Fidelity (or faithfulness): telling the truth, keeping actual and implied
   promises, and meeting contractual agreements.
2. Reparation: making up for the wrongs we have done to others.
3. Gratitude: recognizing what others have done for us and extending our
   gratitude to them.
4. Justice: preventing the improper distribution of good and bad that is not
   in keeping with what people merit or deserve.
5. Beneficence: helping to improve the condition of others in the areas of
   virtue, intelligence, and happiness.

6. Self-improvement: the obligation we have to improve our own virtue, intelligence, and happiness.
7. Nonmaleficence (noninjury): not injuring others and preventing injury to others (21–22).

Wagner (1996) has suggested that teachers (and educational administrators) are entrusted with educating the next generation, and so have the following special duties. One might take the position that these duties (and others that might be identified) take precedence over those considered *prima facie*.

1. Duty to students—teachers are responsible for helping students learn not only academic understanding and self-esteem, but social skills and moral responsibilities as well.
2. Duty to colleagues—it is important for teachers to acknowledge duties they have toward one another as members of a professional community. The teacher owes other teachers a special regard. A teacher must be dedicated to ensuring that every teacher enjoys every opportunity to succeed as a teacher.
3. Duty to discipline—teachers must ensure that the integrity of the discipline is maintained throughout the curriculum and never sacrificed to some instructional gimmickry.
4. Duty to the school team—Total Quality Management and site-based management have brought to the fore the concept of a school team. Teammates have a right to depend on each other.
5. Duty to the profession—the profession is greater than the sum of its individual members. Teachers have a duty to honor their profession through what they say and do.
6. Duty to funding sources—those who pay for education have a legitimate claim on the professional teacher.
7. Duty to parents—parents must trust their children to schools and to the stewardship of professional educators.
8. Duty to community—teachers' special duty toward the community is to show students the importance of becoming "community-regarding," that is, to respect the concept of community and to cooperate to bring about good things for the community (12–19).

Justice

We use the term *justice* in a variety of ways, typically without giving much thought to its precise meaning. However, if we are going to use the concept in a system of ethics and procedures for making ethical decisions, we must come to some agreement as to its precise meaning. Some questions that illustrate the challenge in doing this might include the following:

1. Should grades in school be based solely on achievement, as measured by some sort of examination, or should the student's effort be considered?
2. Should handicapped students (including those handicapped by their social and/or home environment) be held to the same requirements for graduation from high school as other students?
3. What kinds of absences from class should be excused? What privileges or penalties should be attached to excused and unexcused absences?
4. Should boys and girls be punished in the same way for misbehavior?
5. Should teacher salaries be based on merit or seniority?
6. Should property owners be the citizens held primarily responsible for providing the necessary funds to operate schools?
7. Should parents be punished by legal authorities for their children's absences from school?
8. Should all students be treated equally for similar behavior?
9. Who should be considered qualified for membership on the school board?
10. Should the federal or state authorities or local school boards be primarily responsible for determining what is taught in schools (relative to the theory of evolution or abortion, for example)?

Definition of Justice.   These kinds of questions show the necessity of a good definition and understanding of the term *justice*. Of course, others have recognized this challenge. MacIntyre (1966) reminds us that Plato wanted to know "what it is about an action or class of actions which leads us to call it just. He wants not a list of just actions, but a criterion for inclusion in or exclusion from such a list" (33). Plato's mentor, Socrates, proposed that "justice is that state of affairs in which everyone has regard to his own concerns." Plato then tried "to show [that] justice is first in the state, and then in the soul. He outlined a state in which all basic needs are met. Three classes of citizens are required: artisans and laborers to produce the material needs of society; soldiers to defend the state; and rulers to organize its social life" (36).

Durant (1953) further explains that Plato went on to propose that justice means "that each man shall receive the equivalent of what he produces, and shall perform the function for which he is best fit. A just man is a man in just the right place, doing his best, and giving the full equivalent of what he receives. A society of just men would be therefore a highly harmonious and efficient group; for every element would be in its place, fulfilling its appropriate function like the pieces in a perfect orchestra. Justice in a society would be like that harmony of relationships whereby the planets are held together in their orderly. . . movement. So organized, a society is fit for survival" (33).

"Justice is not mere strength, but harmonious strength—desires and men falling into that order which constitutes intelligence and organization; justice is not the right of the stronger, but the effective harmony of the whole. It is true that the individual who gets out of the place to which his nature and talents adapt him may for a time seize some profit and advantage; but an inescapable

Nemesis pursues him. . . . the Nature of Things drives the refractory instrument back to its place and its pitch and its natural note" (Durant 1953, 33).

More recent attempts to define justice often use the word *fair* as a descriptor. But that also requires a definition. Walter Lippman proposed that fairness is ". . . what men would choose if they saw clearly, thought rationally, acted disinterestedly and benevolently" (Held 1970, 205, as quoted in Cooper, 1990). Fletcher (1966) suggests that "Love and justice are the same, for justice is love distributed, nothing else" (99). "Justice is Christian love using its head, calculating its duties, obligations, opportunities, and resources. Love does not permit us to solve our problems or soothe our wounds at the expense of innocent third parties. Our neighbors include all our neighbors" (95).

Kinds of Justice. "[Aristotle] distinguishes between distributive justice—fairness—and the corrective justice which is involved in redress for a harm done" (MacIntyre 1966, 33). He basically identifies two kinds of justice—the lawful and the fair (378). More recently, additional kinds of justice (or injustice) have been identified by Chryssides and Kaler (1996).

1. *Procedural justice*, which ". . . deals with the treatment people ought to receive in connection with the application of rules that govern or control them in some way. It is about applying those rules in a consistent and even-handed way. The fundamental principles . . . are said to be enshrined in the maxims, 'Hear the other side. . .' and, 'No one shall be judge in one's own case' (judgment must be impartial)" (45–46).
2. *Substantive justice*, that goes beyond procedure and examines the "rightness" of rules and procedures. It seeks to protect ownership of property, compensation for work, freedom, privacy, bodily safety, truth telling, citizenship, or copyright (46).
3. *Retributive justice*, which ". . . involves punishment for wrong-doing. It concerns what punishment is appropriate for what offence and how to maintain a correct balance between severity and leniency . . . A precondition for retribution is the committing of the relevant offence. . ." (46–47).
4. *Remedial justice*, sometimes called compensatory justice "deals with wrong-doing with respect to the victim, rather than . . . the perpetrator. It involves putting things right, making amends, restoring what was unfairly lost" (47).
5. *Distributive justice*, deals with showing that "there is no necessary connection with wrong-doing. It concerns the way in which benefits and burdens are to be shared out among people. Its aim is the morally correct division of things such as wealth, power, property, obligations" (47).

Principles of Justice. To achieve justice and avoid abuses, such as harsh results, some principles to follow would seem to be helpful. John Rawls (1958), from Abelson and Friquegnon, eds. (1975), who is recognized as one of the more prominent thinkers in the field suggests the following.

"The conception of justice which I want to develop may be stated in the form of two principles as follows: first, each person participating in a practice, or affected by it, has an equal right to the most extensive liberty compatible with a like liberty for all; and second, inequalities are arbitrary unless it is reasonable to expect that they will work out for everyone's advantage, and provided the positions and offices to which they attach or from which they may be gained, are open to all. These principles express justice as a complex of three ideas: liberty, equality, and reward for services contributing to the common good" (523).

"A practice is just or fair. . .when it satisfies the principles which those who participate in it could propose to one another for mutual acceptance . . .Persons engaged in a just, or fair. . . practice can face one another openly and support their respective positions, should they appear questionable, by reference to principles which it is reasonable to expect each to accept" (532).

"Acting fairly requires more than simply being able to follow rules; what is fair must often be felt, or perceived, . . . it is usually considered unfair if someone accepts the benefits of a practice but refuses to do his part in maintaining it" (533).

Potential Abuses.   In the name of justice, many injustices occur. Two of the most common involve the equal treatment of nonequals or the unequal treatment of equals, a danger identified by Aristotle and many others since his time. Unreasonably harsh results or failure to achieve justice due to legal technicalities may also be cited as potential abuses. Also, if carried too far, attempts to provide needed services for those with special needs may result in failure to adequately meet the needs of others. Adequate attention to principles from Rawls and others will help us avoid these and other potential abuses of attempts to achieve justice in our society.

Equity

The terms *justice* and *equity* are often considered somewhat synonymous, but Aristotle (*Nicomachean Ethics*) and others since his time have recognized the need to give further consideration to situations where laws and recognized practices result in unfair treatment if followed without question or adjustment. In somewhat obtuse fashion, he stated the problem as follows.

What creates the problem is that the equitable is just, but not the legally just but a correction of legal justice. The reason is that all law is universal but about some things it is not possible to make a universal statement which shall be correct. In those cases, then, in which it is necessary to speak universally, but not possible to do so correctly, the law takes the usual case, though it is not ignorant of the possibility of error. And it is nonetheless correct, for the error is not in the law nor in the legislator but in the nature of the thing, since the matter of practical affairs is of this kind from the start. When the law speaks universally, then, and a case arises on it which is not covered by the universal statement, then it is right, where the legislator fails us and has erred by over simplicity, to correct the omission—to say what the legislator himself would have said had he been present, and would have put into his law if he had known. Hence the equitable is just, and better than one kind of justice—not better than absolute justice but better than the error that rises from the absoluteness of the statement. And this is the nature of the equitable, a correction of law where it is defective owing to its universality. . . when the thing is indefinite the rule also is indefinite, like the leaden rule used in making the Lesbian molding; the rule adapts itself to the shape of the stone and is not rigid, and so too the decree is adapted to the facts.

It is plain, then what the equitable is, and that it is just and is better than one kind of justice. It is evident also from this who the equitable man is; the man who chooses and does such acts, and is no stickler for his rights in a bad sense but tends to take less than his share though he has the law on his side, is equitable, and this state of character is equity, which is a sort of justice and not a different state of character (386).

Equity, then, becomes "bending the rules" to fit the situation. This, again, falls under the principle of treating equals equally and nonequals unequally, but not to the point of becoming unfair. Two directions this discussion may take are in the areas of equal opportunity and egalitarianism.

Equal opportunity is a prominent point of discussion and action relative to current political, economic, and educational issues. For example, applying the same standardized test score requirements for admission to a university or consideration for scholarships may be unfair to one whose native language is not English or to one whose cultural background is different from that on which the test is based. To do so may also create inaccurate results (prediction of academic success). Certain individuals, therefore, do not have an equal opportunity to succeed in life. Practices related to equal opportunity may range from the extremes of traditional racial or cultural discrimination to giving preference to certain groups by means of quotas or other arbitrary policies developed as a result of "affirmative action." Chryssides and Kaler (1996) have identified a "spectrum of approaches" to discrimination which may be followed, from

1. Traditional discrimination to
2. Non-discrimination to
3. Positive action without targets to
4. Positive action with targets to
5. Preference for underrepresented groups where equally able, to
6. Preference for underrepresented groups even where less able (91).

Egalitarianism goes even further than "equal opportunity" concerning human rights, maintaining that there are rights held equally by all human beings. This is contrary to ideas that some rights are reserved for those who deserve them because of heredity, natural ability, hard work, etc. If one follows the egalitarianism argument far enough, it will lead to a socialistic society. On the other hand, if it is ignored, we will have a *laissez-faire* society. Again, we are left with the question, "What is ethical?"

Case Studies

A Testing Situation

Kantra Versal joined the staff as an assistant principal four years ago. She was very skilled as an assistant principal, with a strong background in curriculum and an ability to effectively assist teachers with discipline management. She was recognized as an outstanding talent by her staff and was very popular among staff members and the community.

Prior to Ms. Versal's arrival, the school was known as a low performing campus. There was violence, racial turmoil, widespread parental discontent, and extremely low test scores. The board demanded that something be done. As superintendent, your answer, after many telephone calls from teachers and parents, was to promote Ms. Versal to the principalship. With her strong support among parents and students and evident talent, you felt sure you had made the right decision.

The following year the school showed an amazing improvement. Teachers were innovative and initiated several very effective improvement programs. In a year's time, Ms. Versal managed to get the staff and parents focused and involved in school improvement. Telephone calls about the school were different this year. Parents, board members, and staff shared their compliments of the job Ms. Versal was doing and of your ability to "save the education of over 2000 students." This was one fire that seemed, as it turned out, to have benefited your image and career as an effective superintendent.

Key to Ms. Versal's strategy for school improvement was to empower the teachers (through the Campus Improvement Council) and the Student Council. They were very active in the improvement process. As part of Drug Free Schools Week, an activity was planned in the late spring. Both groups decided to initiate a volunteer drug testing program for students. The Campus Improvement Council (which included a board member) showed their support by committing all staff members to be tested, also. The staff agreed to be tested and, as an act of commitment to drug-free schools, agreed to let all results be sent to you. This school was on the cutting edge of improvement and was setting a precedent for other schools to follow.

This morning, one day after the project was announced on her campus, Ms. Versal walked into your office and informed you that she had a drug problem that, according to her, she "is trying to kick." She requested that you prevent any kind of test that might risk her problem being "discovered." She also requested that you inform the staff that, while there is no policy to prevent it, there would be no drug testing. Finally, she informed you that she told the faculty the testing project would require your approval and that the faculty wanted a decision in time for the faculty meeting tomorrow morning at 7:30 a.m. Ms. Versal thanked you for your understanding and for your support.

As you consider what to do you are sure that the board would want to know why there would be no testing.

Questions to Consider

1. Ms. Versal has been what her staff and students needed. Exposing the truth about her problem will result in her removal. What is best for the students and staff of the school that have grown and improved under her leadership?
2. What responsibility do you have to the staff, students, parents, and board members? What responsibility do you have to Ms. Versal? Do the responsibilities conflict with each other or with principles of fairness and justice?
3. Regardless of what decision is made about the drug testing, should you do something about Ms. Versal's drug use and her appointment as principal? If so, what? Do legal issues and school district policies impact the situation?
4. What are some alternative measures you might take other than to cancel the drug testing?
5. Does Ms. Versal have rights that deserve protection in this case? Are one or more of them forfeited due to her responsibilities?
6. Do issues of fairness and justice conflict in this situation? If so, which should prevail in your decisions and actions?
7. If you "cover" for Ms. Versal now, is this likely to be discovered later—to your professional harm? Should this question even enter into your thinking?

Alternative Lifestyle

Ms. Jones is a teacher and coach in Troublesome I.S.D. Although she is relatively new to the district, she has proved herself to be both competent and dedicated to her students. She is well-respected among her colleagues, and the students think highly of her as well. However, Ms. Jones is not like most other teachers; she is gay, and she has a female friend with whom she lives.

As word begins to spread that Ms. Jones is "different," her colleagues pay no mind simply because they indicate "they knew all along . . . now it's just confirmed." However, the students aren't quite sure what to think of this. In fact, many students begin to find humor in ridiculing and harassing the teacher, both verbally and in writing. Parents begin calling the school requesting to have their child removed from Ms. Jones's class simply because they do not agree with her choice of lifestyle.

Mr. Jackson, the school principal, is once again feeling pressure. While Ms. Jones is a good teacher, the fact that she is different is causing problems among students and parents, and many of them want her out. On the other hand, Ms. Jones maintains that she has rights, too; she has the right to work in an environment where she is not harassed and ridiculed, especially since she is very careful to keep her private life separate from her professional life (Contributed by Jodi Duron).

Questions to Consider

1. Does Ms. Jones have the right to maintain her preferred lifestyle without harassment or danger to her teaching career?
2. Do parents have the right to choose who will teach their children?
3. Is it fair to require different standards of conduct for teachers than are required of other public servants? If so, who should be responsible for deciding what these standards are and what criteria will be followed to define such standards?
4. Is the school principal responsible for maintaining standards of conduct for teachers, or should this be left to the school board and/or legal authorities?
5. Should students be free to express their feelings relative to the lifestyle or other characteristics of teachers (or other students)?
6. Do teachers' responsibilities to students, the community, and society put special limits on their rights and freedoms?
7. This case doesn't speak to the sexual preferences of students, but what rights and freedoms do students have in this regard?

Basketball Blues

On a Sunday afternoon in February, you, a high school principal, received a telephone call from Pam Smith, the girls' varsity basketball coach. Coach Smith told you she had just had a visit from one of the varsity players and her parents. The player told Coach Smith that five of the varsity girls' basketball team players had been stealing items from locker rooms during away games since December. Two of the players are starters. Currently, the team is undefeated and has only two games remaining in district competition. The team should win the district championship and has an excellent chance to go far in play-off competition. The toughest game of the season is this coming Tuesday night.

Coach Smith says one sophomore, one junior, and three seniors are involved. Ms. Gorman tells the coach she wants the coach to meet with the three assistant principals who are responsible for those grade levels, the campus athletic coordinator, and Ms. Gorman at 7:00 a.m. Monday morning to relate the details of everything the player told Coach Smith.

Following the meeting with Coach Smith on Monday morning, Ms. Gorman, the campus athletic coordinator, and the three assistant principals decided how to conduct the investigation. Following the questioning of the individual players, the administrators reconvened to share information and to determine a course of action. Four of the players admitted they had stolen items and enumerated what those items were. The fifth girl, a senior, said she had not stolen anything, but that one of the other four had given her a CD, which she took home to copy and then returned to the girl. The stories of the four girls who confessed to stealing things were corroborated by each other. The problem was the four players also said the senior who denied stealing was very much aware she had stolen property and should suffer the same punishment. However, no one could produce the missing CD, and the assistant principal who interviewed the senior believed her story.

Ms. Gorman stressed the importance of consistency among the three assistant principals in determining the consequences for the girls. The administrators decided that the four girls who confessed should receive six days in In School Suspension (ISS) and the senior who admitted to copying the stolen CD should serve two days in In School Suspension for knowingly handling stolen property and not reporting it. While in ISS the girls would not be allowed to play in the remaining two district games. Ms. Gorman stated that the ISS assignment should begin immediately the next day, a game day, and all principals should notify the parents that afternoon before leaving school.

Following this meeting, two of the assistant principals were overheard by a teacher discussing the investigation and stating they did not agree with the consequences. Ms. Gorman was also informed by the coach the next day (game day) that the assistant principal for the senior class had not put the senior who copied the CD in ISS immediately, so therefore she would be able to compete in the game that evening.

No charges were filed against any of the girls because none of the schools from which items were stolen wanted to press charges as long as all the items were returned. The girls were instructed to return all stolen articles immediately.

This was a high profile incident, and word spread quickly about the punishment. Reactions were varied. Coach Smith knew the girls had to be punished, but was frustrated they had to sit out the last two games of district competition. Ms. Gorman had two parent conferences. The parents of the girl who first disclosed the information to Coach Smith told Ms. Gorman the consequences were appropriate, but they felt all the girls should have received exactly the same punishment, regardless of their degree of involvement. They argued that if consideration was given to the senior who copied the stolen CD, then their daughter also should receive less punishment because she had been the one to come forward with the information initially. The parents of the senior who had taken the stolen CD home to copy were appreciative that the administration had recognized that their daughter's involvement was "second-hand." The reaction among faculty members was mixed (Contributed by Sandy Mossman).

Questions to Consider

1. What consideration, if any, should be given to the players who confessed?
2. Should the player who first reported the thefts be given less punishment?
3. Should all the players be treated equally?
4. How should Ms. Gorman handle the action of the assistant principal that failed to put the senior in ISS the next day, which resulted in the girl being able to play in the game that evening?
5. What action should Ms. Gorman take regarding the two assistant principals who were overheard discussing the situation in the hallway?
6. What should you do as the principal if you personally feel the senior class assistant principal made an error in judgment, but you have told the assistant principals the decision on how to discipline the players will be made by the entire administrative staff and they have agreed on how to handle the situation?

Activities and Discussion Questions _____

1. Review the Bill of Rights from the United States Constitution and discuss educators' professional rights that may be implied.

2. Which rights that might be advocated by parents, students, or educators do you consider *prima facie* and which ones do you consider absolute?

3. Which rights of students would be considered positive and which ones would be considered negative?

4. Identify some of the controversial positive rights which parents and/or students might consider important.

5. From a student "code of conduct," identify students whose freedom is limited and those whose freedom is protected by its standards.

6. What does the saying "your freedom ends where my nose begins" mean to you as related to your work as an educator? Identify at least three sets of conflicting freedoms in an educational setting.

7. What are the limits to students' and/or teachers' freedom of speech?

8. When is it morally right to violate someone's rights or freedom?

9. Identify some situations where you believe it would be morally right to "bend the rules." What are the dangers in doing this?

10. Describe some situations in your professional experience in which "equity" has been confused with "equality."

11. Identify some situations in which you have experienced a conflict between equity and consistency in applying school policies or rules. How do you reconcile these conflicts?

12. Describe some situations where school leaders may encounter a conflict between equity and justice.

13. Plato said that each person should receive the equivalent of what he or she produces. Is this "fair" in relation to disabled or handicapped persons? What about those "born into money"?

14. Interview a female school administrator regarding the barriers women face in advancement to administrative positions and in functioning as educational administrators.

15. What is the relationship between responsibility and freedom?

16. Plato states that "justice is not the right of the stronger, but the effective harmony of the whole." What are the implications of this statement in educational settings?

17. With which kinds of justice, as described in this chapter, are educators most likely to be concerned?

18. Several definitions of justice are given in this chapter. Write your own definition and explain why you like it better than those given.

19. Describe an instance in which you believe that you were not given equal opportunity. How did you feel about this? What do you think would have been a more ethical approach to the situation?

20. Show how responsibilities of educational leaders imply certain duties.

21. Does the word "duty" have a somewhat negative tone to you? Why might this be true?

22. What does the phrase "duty for duty's sake" mean to you?

23. Show how certain responsibilities of a school administrator might at times conflict with each other.

24. Educators like to say, "We do what's best for the children." However, there are situations where what is best for some children obviously is not best for all children. Identify at least three such situations that exist today.

25. Do you support the concept that nonequals should not be treated equally? Discuss some implications of this principle for educators. In what ways is it often violated?

References

Abelson, R. and Friquegnon, M., eds. (1975). Ethics for modern life. New York: St. Martin's Press.

Aristotle. Nicomachean ethics. The works of Aristotle, vol. II, Great books of the western world. In Hutchins, R. M., ed. (1952). Chicago: Encyclopedia Britannica.

Barnard, C. I. (1964). *The function of the executive*. Cambridge, MA: Harvard University Press.

Barrow, R. (1975). *Moral philosophy for education*. London: Allen & Unwin.

Chryssides, G. and Kaler, J. (1996). *Essentials of business ethics*. London: McGraw-Hill.

Cooper, T. L. (1990). *The responsible administrator: An approach to ethics for the administrative role (3rd ed)*. San Francisco: Jossey-Bass.

Durant, W. (1953). *The story of philosophy*. New York: Simon and Schuster.

Fletcher, J. (1966). *Situation ethics*. Philadelphia: The Westminster Press.

Harwood, S. (1993). Introduction: Basic definitions of five major moral theories. In Pojman, L. P., ed. *Moral Philosophy: A Reader*. (141–154). Indianapolis: Hackett Publishing.

Held, V. (1970). *The public interest and individual interests*. New York: Basic Books.

Ladd, E. C. (1995). *Individualism, strength or weakness?* In Wekesser, C., ed. *Ethics*. San Diego, CA: Greenhaven Press.

MacIntyre, A. (1966). *A short history of ethics*. New York: Macmillan.

Ottensmeyer, E. J. and McCarthy, G D. (1996). *Ethics in the workplace*. New York: McGraw-Hill.

Pojman, L. P. (2002). *Ethics: Discovering right and wrong* (4th ed.). Belmont, CA: Wadsworth Publishing Company.

Rawls, J. (1958). Justice as fairness. *The Philosophical Review, vol. LXVII*. (522–542.)

Ross, W. D. (1930). *The right and the good*. New York: Oxford University Press.

Scott, B. R. and Wong, K. L. (1996). *Beyond integrity: A Judeo-Christian approach to business ethics*. Grand Rapids, MI: Zondervan Publishing House.

Thiroux, J. (1998). *Ethics: Theory and practice* (6th ed.). Upper Saddle River, NJ: Prentice Hall.

Wagner, P. A. (1996). *Understanding professional ethics*. Bloomington, IN: Phi Delta Kappa Educational Foundation.

Section

II

Ethical Theories and Philosophical Domains for Assessing Actions

As discussed in Chapter 1, our first task in developing a philosophy and ethical system we can live by, one that will enable us to make the best decisions in difficult situations, is to identify the ultimate goal of our actions. What is the measure of a good life? And what guides to our actions and decisions may best produce that good life? Aristotle, according to Adler and Cain (1962), answered this question by saying that the good life is the happy life, but he went on to define happiness in larger terms than is typical today.

For Aristotle, happiness is man's highest good, the end to which all human activities contribute when properly performed. Happiness is attained through the satisfaction of all human needs and through the perfection of all of man's natural faculties (37).

Aristotle's ideas are then contrasted with those from Aquinas and Hobbes. Aquinas elaborates on Aristotle by suggesting that there must be "one last end of human life" (Adler and Cain 1962, 95), an absolute, universal good to which all lesser ends or goods are directed as man's final goal and fulfillment. Aquinas calls this last end "happiness, . . . and links it concretely, in its objective content, with the God of Biblical faith . . . and the beginning and end of all things" (Adler and Cain 1962, 95). Aquinas argues that. . . "whatever happiness may be, it certainly cannot consist in such imperfect, finite, or merely instrumental things as material wealth, public honor and acclaim, political or social power, bodily health, sensual pleasure, or even the goods of the soul, such as the limited knowledge and wisdom that man can attain in this life" (Adler and Cain 1962, 95). The conclusion of Aquinas' answer leads back to a Biblical text from the First Epistle of John: "When He shall appear, we shall be like to Him, and we shall see Him as He is" (Adler and Cain 1962, 97).

Hobbes, on the other hand, places his faith in science and human reason, relying on the model of mathematics and the physical sciences as they depend on the human senses to develop understanding (Adler and Cain 1962, 107–111).

Of these three prominent philosophers and all the others we might study, whose ideas are best? If "happiness" of some type is the ultimate goal of life, how should it be defined? If "happiness" is not the right word to use for such a large task, what word or words might be better—and how should they be defined?

The "big questions" of life, including those related to what we call ethics, have been studied and written about by philosophers. We won't attempt a detailed study of philosophy, but we will rely on those considered among the best thinkers of the past and present to help us develop a workable approach to the study and application of ethical principles in life and in educational leadership.

As you seek answers to difficult questions or the best action to take when confronted with a difficult dilemma, there may not be a sure way of always coming to the best conclusion. Neither may there be any one best way to proceed. But by understanding the basic theories from the study of philosophy and ethics, and understanding the options they offer, you may at least be able to recognize the relevant factors to be considered and then choose what seems to be the best course of action. The study of philosophy and ethics will provide a more orderly, more thoughtful approach to solving problems in educational leadership than the typical tendency to "do what has always been done" or "fly by the seat of your pants."

This section will introduce the major ethical theories and show how they differ in proposed ways to achieve the "good" life. The moral order is typically viewed as either **changing** or **absolute**, with variations on those themes, and we will explore the major approaches (or theories) to moral understanding which have been developed by those who tend to follow one approach or the other.

After each theory is described, you will examine "guides to action" related to that theory. These guides help you to use a particular theory to decide what action to take and how actions should be evaluated. Objectivism, for instance, relies primarily on deontology (rules). Relativism uses as its guide to action the consequences or probable consequences of action options. Axiology (value theory) depends on motive (as determined by character and guided by what is considered most "valuable" in life) to guide and evaluate action. A variation or enlargement of value theory may be seen in those who advocate a "theory of care."

References _____

Adler, M. and Cain, S. (1962). *Ethics: The study of moral values.* Chicago: Encyclopedia Britannica.

3

Objectivism and Deontology

*After several years of very successful teaching experience and appropriate
graduate school study, Yolanda was into her second day as a new
elementary school assistant principal when she encountered a formidable
dilemma. The new "zero tolerance" policy of her school district prescribed
automatic "in-school suspension" for a student caught with a knife in their
possession. Johnny's family was new to the district, and this was his second
day in first grade. The lunchroom supervisor noticed that Johnny was
using a small knife to cut the apple his mother had sent in his lunch.
Following school policy, she brought Johnny to Yolanda for disciplinary
action.*

The Ethical Theory of Moral Objectivism

Probably the most widely held and easiest to describe beliefs about ethics fall
into the group of approaches typically labeled **moral objectivism**. Moral
objectivism takes the position that moral principles have objective validity,
independent of cultural acceptance. These principles have universal and largely
unchanging application. Nash (1996) explains this as follows. "Objectivists . . .
believe that knowledge, to be secure, must rest on indubitable premises that take
on the character of bedrock certainties. Objectivists maintain that moral truths
exist prior to and apart from observation and thought, and it is the project of all
human beings to discover these mind-independent realities" (49).

It may be that a person does not fully understand how a moral principle
should be applied, but is still obligated to follow it as best they can. The moral
principles or rules ("commandments," if you please) will serve as good reasons
and the best guidance for making practical decisions.

Kidder (1995) calls this approach to making difficult decisions "rules-based thinking." Actions should be guided, according to this way of thinking, by standards that are established by deciding if the action would be one which all people should follow and which would produce the greatest good. Actions are based firmly on duty, what one ought to do, not on what might work or possibly produce the best results. One must not "open the gate" of a moral position or rule, because there may develop too much temptation and the likelihood of unavoidable pressure to randomly violate the rule or principle.

There are close connections between moral objectivism and authoritarian approaches to leadership in organizations. After all, if there are universal rules that should be followed, why is there any need for democratic processes or shared decision making? The leader simply needs a good knowledge of law and established or generally accepted rules and the will to follow them. If input is encouraged or accepted from the led it is primarily to facilitate good morale or good human relations in order to improve motivation of employees and subordinates.

Objectivism relies on either divine law or natural law to define basic principles. Divine law comes from some accepted supernatural source (God), while natural law (Aquinas, Hobbes, et al.) is discovered through human reason and observation of the nature of humanity and society. Natural law defines universal rules, just as does divine law, including the following key ideas, as suggested by Pojman (2002).

1. Human beings have an essential rational nature established by God, who designed us to live and flourish in prescribed ways (from Aristotle and the Stoics).
2. Even without knowledge of God, reason, as the essence of our nature, can discover the laws that are necessary for human flourishing (from Aristotle; developed by Aquinas).
3. The natural laws are universal and unchangeable, and one should use them to judge individual societies and their positive laws. Positive (or actual) laws of societies that are not in line with the natural law are not truly laws but counterfeits (from the Stoics) (45).

Kant, the most prominent theoretician subscribing to the objectivist viewpoint, was devoutly religious and maintained that there could be no difference between valid religious ethics and valid philosophical or natural ethics. His position was that both God and humanity have to obey the same rational principles, and reason is sufficient to guide us to these principles (Pojman 2002, 153).

When applying objectivist principles, there is a need to distinguish between **moral absolutism** and **moral objectivism.** Although they share a common approach to morality, the absolutist believes there are nonoverridable moral principles that ought never to be violated, no matter what the consequences of following those principles may be. The objectivist shares with the absolutist the notion that moral principles have universal, objective validity, but denies that moral norms are necessarily exceptionless. According to this view, each moral principle has to be weighed against other moral principles.

The moral absolutist would maintain that it is wrong to lie under any circumstances, simply because truth telling is an absolute requirement for moral living. This sometimes leads to disturbing consequences, such as when there is the need to protect an innocent person from persecution or death because of their ethnicity or political persuasion. If such a person is in hiding, you know where the person is, and the persecuting authorities ask you if you know of the person's whereabouts (as in the case of Anne Frank), a moral dilemma is obvious. A moral absolutist would maintain that no deviation from the truth is acceptable, even to protect a person from probable persecution. The moral objectivist solves this dilemma and would lie to protect the innocent. How would lying be justified? By maintaining that the principle of protecting innocent human life overrides the principle of truth telling—thereby allowing protection of Anne Frank by lying about her hiding place.

Moral absolutists usually moderate their stance by accepting the **principle of double effect** to accommodate those dilemmas in which following a principle without exception will result in evil consequences. As described by Pojman (2002), this doctrine provides a way to follow the absolutist approach, which would result in both good and bad consequences, by saying

> it is always wrong to do a bad act intentionally in order to bring about good consequences, but that it is sometimes permissible to do a good act despite knowing that it will bring about bad consequences. This doctrine consists in four conditions that must all be satisfied before an act is morally permissible.
>
> 1. The Nature-of-the-Act Condition: The action must be either morally good or indifferent. Lying or intentionally killing an innocent person are never permissible.
> 2. The Means-End Condition: The bad effect must not be the means by which one achieves the good effect.
> 3. The Right-Intention Condition: The intention must be the achieving of only the good effect, with the bad effect being only an unintended side effect. If the bad effect is a means of obtaining the good effect, then the act is immoral. The bad effect may be foreseen but must not be intended.
> 4. The Proportionality Condition: The good effect must be at least equivalent in importance to the bad effect (45–46).

According to this doctrine, a doctor may give pain-killing drugs to a patient who would otherwise die in agony, although as a side effect his death is accelerated, but he must not give a drug that will kill the patient as a way of preventing further pain. Also, a man defending himself against an attacker may do something that has two effects: the saving of his own life and the death of the attacker. However, lying under any circumstances, even the probable saving of innocent human life, is not permissible.

Action Guide: Deontology

If one subscribes to the objective approach to ethics and moral action, then the system used to determine and evaluate actions is one which may be described as "nonconsequential"—the deontological system. The term *deontology* comes from the Greek words *deon*, meaning "duty," and *logos*, meaning "logic." With this system of thinking, the focus of value is the act or kind of act (Pojman 2002, 107). Consequences of actions are not important when it comes to deciding what is right and wrong. According to the nonconsequentialist, "the most important thing to remember . . . is that . . . consequences do not, and in fact should not, enter into judging whether actions or people are moral or immoral. Actions are to be judged solely on whether they are right and people solely on whether they are good, based on some other (many nonconsequentialists would say 'higher') standard or standards of morality" (Thiroux 1998, 56). The end never justifies the means.

Variations

Variations on the deontological concept are of two general types—act- and rule-deontology. As explained by Pojman (2002), **act-deontologists** "see each act as a unique ethical occasion and believe that we must decide on what is right or wrong in each situation by consulting our conscience or our intuitions or by making a choice apart from any rules" (135). This approach may lead so far as to propose, as do the existentialists, that "there is no morally right answer until we choose for ourselves what is right and what is wrong" (135). This theory is characterized by two popular slogans from the 1960s: "If it feels good, do it" and "Do your own thing" (Thiroux 1998, 57). In many respects, act-deontology is very similar in action to various forms of relativism or consequentialist theory, which will be discussed later.

Act-deontologists do not give us much guidance in attempting to suggest consistent actions or develop binding moral principles. **Rule-deontologists** are more specific (and more aligned with what we usually think of when we follow deontological ideas), maintaining that it is one's duty to act according to unchanging principles. The only difficulty in deciding how to act morally is in figuring out what the basic principles should be—and many times this no small task.

The philosopher most identified with rule-deontology is Immanuel Kant, who lived from 1724 to 1804. Even though most people may not be familiar with his name, they are likely to follow his general approach to determining morality and moral action. As pointed out by MacIntyre (1966), to many "morality is roughly what Kant said it was" (190).

Rule-deontology maintains that we cannot rely on our natural inclinations to determine moral action, because natural inclinations are often motivated by personal gain or questionable custom. We must choose between our natural inclination and duty. But how do we know what our duty is? Again quoting MacIntyre, duty "presents itself as obedience to a law that is universally binding on all rational beings. I become aware of [this law] as a set of precepts which in prescribing to myself I can consistently will should be obeyed by all rational beings" (193). Kant called such precepts *categorical imperatives.* Freedom thus takes on new meaning, "for it is only in acts of obedience to the categorical imperative that we are delivered from the bondage of our own inclinations" (196).

Kant proposes that nothing is unconditionally good except a good will. The performance of acts considered good do not make a person good—unless they are accompanied by a good will. And a good will is motivated by a person's devotion to duty. An act is good because a person does it out of a sense of duty to do what is considered right according to universal principles. Honesty in business dealings, for instance, is not considered good if the person's motivation is simply to build good will and more business. Honesty is good only if it is motivated by a sense of duty and the obligation to do the right thing that ensues. "The good will's only motive is to do its duty for the sake of doing its duty" (MacIntyre 1966, 192).

Kant held to the belief that universal maxims (categorical imperatives) can be realized by man through his powers of reason, although they are of divine origin. The typical examples of categorical imperatives tell us what not to do (not to break promises, tell lies, commit suicide or murder, etc.), but they aren't very specific as to what we *should* do. The categorical imperative, expressed by Kant in several ways, simply says that an act is immoral if a rule authorizing it cannot be made into a rule for all human beings to follow. Stated in reverse, as in the Golden Rule, it asks if a person would want a rule behind an action to apply to him or her.

Another basic principle from Kant, the "principle of ends," states that one should "so act as to treat humanity, whether in your own person or in that of any other, in every case as an end and never as merely a means" (Pojman 2002, 149). This concept is included as one of the requirements for use of the "principle of double effect" previously described.

A review of the discussion of duty in Chapter 2 may help you develop a better understanding of rule-consequentialism and the "duties of duty."

Arguments for and against Objectivism and Deontology

Arguments *for* moral objectivity and deontology include the following:

1. Because they are "objective," their principles don't rely on individual interpretation for validity. Therefore, they are relatively easy to understand

and to follow, including the development of corollaries and rules to implement the basic principles. "Right" and "wrong" usually are not hard to recognize.

2. The principles to be followed have been developed because of common human needs and following them also helps maintain continuity in society and prevent undesirable changes. This argument turns consideration of cultural and other human differences, which is used to justify relativism (see Chapter 4), to the position that since there are so many differences, we need a set of universals, because who is to judge right and wrong? We must not argue that simply because most members of a group or social system believe something is right that it is necessarily so.

3. If any set of beliefs is acceptable because of legitimate human differences, how can one argue the need for reform? The idea of moral reform becomes self-contradictory.

4. In its simplest form, the argument for objectivity by those who believe that God is the source of their moral principles simply states that "we can't argue with God."

5. We tend to be more comfortable with a set of rules than with the challenge of deciding day by day what is right and wrong. This lends itself to a system of laws and a more orderly society. The status quo is more easily maintained, and those who are favored by a particular system of rules and laws like to keep it that way.

Arguments *against* moral objectivity include the following:

1. The source of the accepted basic principles, be they a supreme being or "natural law," is questionable.

2. It is difficult to distinguish unforeseen from unintended consequences (when trying to use the doctrine of double effect).

3. Nothing in this world is unchanging and universal. Cultural and personal differences make moral objectivism both impractical and irrational.

4. They may lead to thoughtless (indeed mindless) maintenance of rules and practices which have been developed to fit an earlier form of civilization, one which is basically unfair in ways which become obvious to a more advanced society. Reform becomes difficult, if not impossible, except through revolution.

5. A very practical difficulty develops with nonconsequential moral systems when one basic principle comes into conflict with another. Which rule should prevail, for instance, when the preservation of human life conflicts with telling the truth, as in the case of Anne Frank? Or, is it permissible to kill another person in self-defense? Perhaps Kant and his followers would agree that in these kinds of situations a rule might be "qualified" if that qualification applies to everyone (Thiroux 1998, 64).

Case Studies

A Question of Duty

Metropolitan Independent School District is an urban school district facing the challenges of many urban districts—crumbling facilities, budget cutbacks of favorite student programs, a large number of teacher vacancies and uncertified teachers, a high dropout rate, poor teacher morale, and numerous cases of student violence.

You are the principal of Martin Luther King, Jr., High School, and you know that the school has had the reputation of being one of the "worst" schools in a less-than-good school district. In fact, you have been unsuccessful in filling twelve permanent teaching positions since you arrived at the school three years ago. However, you and a few dedicated teachers have been diligently working to change the culture of the school into a "safe haven of excellence" where students can be successful.

One of the dedicated teachers who have helped to spearhead this effort has been Mrs. Queno, the physics teacher. When Mrs. Queno first came to the school two years ago, she only had one physics class, because students were simply terrified of the word "physics." But she has single-handedly turned this program around. She has given up her weekends and evenings to tutor her students on their assignments, coached teams in academic competitions, and even helped her students design their first robot for a state robotics competition. The students love her and are now excited about learning physics.

During the last month, however, you have noticed that Mrs. Queno has been distracted. She has missed several faculty meetings and has not been available for tutoring in over two weeks. Her students have come to you asking why Mrs. Queno has not had meetings with the Robotics Club, and you have even seen her crying softly in the teacher workroom. When you tried to question her, Mrs. Queno mumbled something and quickly left the room.

You decided to talk to Mrs. Queno and went to her room after school. She was talking to another teacher in the hall when you arrived, so you went in her room to wait. While standing near her desk, you noticed an official notice on her desk saying that her five-year visitor's visa had expired two years ago. You then decided to leave the room and investigate further before talking to Mrs. Queno, telling her that you needed to go back to the office.

Upon checking with immigration officials and the social security office in Washington, you found that the social security number Mrs. Queno has been giving to the school district does not exist and that, indeed, her visitor's visa has expired. The immigration office had lost contact with Mrs. Queno and assumed that she had left the country. She has been giving a false social security number to the school district in order to keep her teaching position and stay in the United States. You now know that Mrs. Queno has forged a social security number and is an undocumented immigrant working in your school. It is unlikely that she will be able to stay in the country legally while trying to get a permanent visa (Contributed by Pam Twymon).

Questions to Consider

1. How would you handle this matter? Is it your duty to report Mrs. Queno to the proper authorities, or should you do what you know would be best for Mrs. Queno and her students by "forgetting" about the matter? In other words, does your duty to the students relative to their educational well being override your duty to report illegal activity?
2. Since no one has asked you about Mrs. Queno's immigration status and you first learned about the situation by inadvertently reading her private correspondence, does this alter your obligation to "duty"?
3. Is failing to report an unlawful act the same as lying about it?
4. Should the consequences of your actions be considered as you reach a decision about what to do?
5. Does the principle of double effect apply in this case?

Trial by Test

Robin Robbins is a newly appointed assistant principal who has been known throughout her teaching and administrative career as a very caring person who always tries to do what is best for students. She particularly has a heart for the students who are having difficulty achieving and goes out of her way to help the "underdog." She tutors, volunteers to sponsor students who cannot afford to participate in extra-curricular activities, and teaches a class of students who have not yet passed the state required test, some after numerous attempts. Her assignment is to work with juniors and seniors, and a particular concern of hers is the fact that these students, under state law, will not be allowed to graduate from high school if they do not pass the state-mandated examination.

Ms. Robbins disagrees with the testing system that is in place and feels it is highly unfair to withhold a diploma because of a single test score, knowing that some students are just not good at taking standardized tests. She believes that if a student has earned the credits, they have earned the right to a diploma. Nevertheless, Ms. Robbins knows that this is the system in place now and she is determined to help as many students as she can to master this test and graduate.

Nick is a senior and the sole support for his widowed mother, who is unable to work herself due to medical problems. Nick and his mother are very close, and Nick is determined to finish high school in order to make a better life for his mother and himself. He has managed to stay in school and pass his courses with the help of Ms. Robbins and other teachers who tutor and mentor him as needed. He works after school and on weekends, often until late at night in order to supplement his mother's social security income. The whole faculty knows how difficult life is for Nick and how proud he is and determined to succeed. He is capable, but he seems to have developed a mental block when it comes to math. No matter how hard he tries, Nick cannot pass the math portion of the state test. He has taken the test every time it is offered, but each time he takes it he fails, usually by just a few points. It is now the last opportunity Nick has to pass the test in time to graduate with his class. He has the credits to graduate, but must pass the state math test.

Ms. Robbins and several teachers are committed to helping Nick. Since he has to work and cannot stay after school for tutoring, they have worked with him whenever possible—on weekends, before school, and during lunch and planning time. They have cheered him on, supported him, and helped him try to overcome his fear of the test. The important test day has arrived, and Ms. Robbins is assigned to administer the test to all seniors who have not yet passed it. Test administrators have all received explicit instructions about testing procedures and what to do if any testing improprieties occur. During the test, the monitor is to observe and make sure all students are following directions and that there is no cheating or inappropriate behavior. If any is observed, they are to immediately take up the student's test and notify the principal, who disqualifies the student from that test.

All students are settled in to take the test after directions have been given to them. Each student is seated in a carrel so that they cannot see each other. Ms. Robbins seats herself at a desk in the front of the room where she has a good view of all the students. The testing period is untimed, so Ms. Robbins settles in for what she is sure will be a lengthy session.

About twenty minutes into the test, Ms. Robbins walks around the room to monitor the students' behavior while they are busy working on the test. All seems to be going well, with all students working diligently. Ms. Robbins returns to her seat at the front of the room, not wanting to cause any distraction to the students. As her eyes sweep around the room, to her horror she sees something she hopes is her imagination. She notices Nick with a sheet of paper under his test booklet. Since students are forbidden to bring anything into the testing room, Ms. Robbins knows that there should be no extra paper on anyone's desk. Nick is unaware of Ms. Robbins watching him. He slips out the paper, on which he has evidently written some formulas and tips Ms. Robbins taught him, and glances at the paper in order to help him solve a problem that has him stumped. Ms. Robbins's heart sinks, as she now is sure that Nick is cheating during the test (Contributed by Nancy McLaughlin).

Questions to Consider

1. Should Ms. Robbins ignore what she sees? To stop Nick now and invalidate his test will mean that he will not graduate next month with his class. There is a real possibility that this will mean that Nick will never graduate, because he is becoming very discouraged and needs to work full time.

2. Should Ms. Robbins take the paper away and allow Nick to continue? After all, he just took the paper out and has not had an opportunity to use it yet, and other students cannot see what is going on.

3. Does the moral obligation to help Nick override the obligation to report any cheating on the state exam? What consideration should be given to the fact that Nick has not had the same advantages many of the other students have had and that he desperately needs to graduate so he can work full time to support himself and his mother?

4. Does the principle of double effect apply here?

5. How would a person who subscribes to the tenets of act-deontology and one who is a rule-deontologist differ in the way they might analyze this situation and make decisions about the optional actions that might be taken?

6. How might a moral absolutist and a moral objectivist think differently about this case?

Activities and Discussion Questions _____

1. State a nonoverridable moral principle (or "categorical imperative"). Describe a situation in which following this principle would result in evil consequences.

2. Interview at least three teachers and ask them to give examples that illustrate a tendency to follow "mindlessly" long-standing, but no longer reasonable, rules and practices in schools.

3. Give an example to illustrate how one would follow act-deontology in a school situation, as contrasted with rule-deontology.

4. How might "devotion to duty" result in negative consequences, either in life or as an educator?

5. Describe a situation in which your duty to follow district and/or state policies might conflict with your duty as a professional educator. How would you decide what to do?

6. Describe at least one situation where you have heard it said, "the ends never justify the means." Was this statement valid?

7. Are there times when you should "argue with God," contrary to what religious objectivists would maintain?

8. Identify at least one example of how laws of society seem to be contrary to natural law (and thus counterfeit).

9. Explain with an example the difference between moral absolutists and moral objectivists.

10. In your own words, state Kant's concept of the categorical imperative.

References

Kidder, R. M. (1995). *How good people make tough choices*. New York: William Morrow and Company.

MacIntyre, A. (1966). *A short history of ethics*. New York: Macmillan.

Nash, R. J. (1996). *Real world ethics*. New York: Teachers College Press.

Pojman, L. (2002). *Ethics: Discovering right and wrong*, (4th ed.). Belmont, CA: Wadsworth Publishing Company.

Thiroux, J. (1998). *Ethics: Theory and practice*, (6th ed.). Upper Saddle River, NJ: Prentice Hall.

4

Relativism and Teleology

The Ethical Theory of Relativism

Relativism, the second major theory from which ethical principles may be drawn, takes its strongest argument from the well-known fact that moral codes vary from one society to another and from one historical period to another. There are also differences among groups of a society and during the same historical period (religious and political groups, for instance, and social or economic classes). There are, to be sure, recognizable similarities in basic moral principles that tend to be true across historical and social lines, but even here there are exceptions. Most social systems forbid cannibalism, for example, but some accept and even value it as a way to honor their deceased elders or shame their enemies. Stealing may be thought wrong unless it is from your enemies. Murder is considered wrong, but then we develop debatable definitions to allow killing that is not considered murder (such as abortion and capital punishment).

Because there are times when following objectivist theories and its rules causes undesirable side effects or requires choosing one rule over another in certain situations, philosophers developed the theory of relativism to guide actions. They suggest that even Jesus followed relativist principles, as when he broke the Sabbath laws in order to do good, saying that "The Sabbath was made for man, not man for the Sabbath" (*The Holy Bible, New International Version* 1973, Mark 2:27).

The more prominent early moral philosophers who developed principles of relativism included David Hume (1711–1776), Jeremy Bentham (1748–1832), and John Stuart Mill (1806–1873). Emboldened by the progress and promises of science and human reason, Hume attempted to construct a theory of ethics based on human experience and psychology rather than divine law or natural law. According to Adler and Cain (1962), he suggested that our basic "moral sentiments" are guided by the "social virtues" of benevolence and justice, which are intended to improve the lot of the human race. Following principles of "public utility," they create happiness in others and pleasure in the moral agent (259).

Following Hume's lead, Bentham pursued practical goals of improving laws and approved practices of the time by developing Hume's principle of utility to pursue egalitarian social ends. Seeing outmoded laws and punishments as primarily for the purpose of maintaining the status quo of social and economic privilege, Bentham proposed changes designed to serve the human good, not so much as a matter of justice but because they would promote more happiness and reduce suffering (Pojman 2002, 108–109).

Bentham suggested that pain and pleasure are primarily responsible for human action. By determining if an action is likely to produce either pain or pleasure one may decide what action to take in order to avoid pain and produce pleasure in one or more other persons—following the principle of "utility." Pleasure is used in a broad sense to include "benefit, advantage, pleasure, and good," or the preventing of "mischief, evil, or unhappiness" to individuals or groups (from Abelson and Friquegnon, eds. 1975, 384).

Bentham also attempted to make ethics quantitative, believing that it is possible to measure the anticipated gain in pleasure or reduction of pain. "The greatest good for the greatest number" was the criterion to be followed, and "the end justifies the means" was the maxim.

But how do we define "good"? Perhaps Moore (1949) does this as well as we can hope for, in saying that "Everyone does in fact understand the question 'Is this good?' . . . as soon as the nature of the problem is clearly understood, there should be little difficulty in advancing so far in analysis. Whenever [a person] thinks of 'intrinsic value,' or says that a thing 'ought to exist,' he has before his mind the unique object—the unique property of things—which I mean by good." Hare (1952) gives some additional help when he says that standards for "goodness" cannot be determined until we have two or more things to compare. Then we use logic, experience, etc. to judge "goodness" (398).

To determine the "greatest good for the greatest number," the value of pleasure or pain to an individual person is to be determined by:

1. Its intensity
2. Its duration
3. Its certainty or uncertainty
4. Its propinquity (nearness in place or time) or remoteness
5. Its fecundity (the chance it has of being followed by sensations of the same kind) (Bentham, in Abelson and Friquegnon, eds., 384).

Some additional explanation of relativism is provided by Kidder (1995, 24) as he contrasts "rule-based thinking," and "ends-based thinking." Utilitarian ends-based thinking requires a kind of cost-benefit analysis to determine who will be hurt, who helped and how to measure the intensity of that help.

Because the assessment of consequences is at the heart of ends-based thinking, utilitarianism or relativism, philosophers also use the term *consequentialism* to designate the type of thinking from which they are derived. Possible results are considered and the one that produces the "most blessing over the greatest range" is chosen (Kidder 1995, 24).

Action Guide: Teleology

At the heart of practices aligned with the theory of relativism is an assessment of consequences, a forecasting of outcomes. Thus the term *consequentialism* is often applied to the kinds of guides to action based on the theory of relativism. Philosophers and ethicists use the term **teleology,** from the Greek word *teleos*, meaning "end" or "issue," because, as explained by Kidder, (1995), "you cannot determine the 'greatest good' without speculating on probable futures" (24). For example, deontologists believe in retribution—that the guilty should be punished in proportion to the gravity of their crime (breaking the rules of society), while teleologists prefer punishment that will serve some deterrent or preventive purpose.

The most common forms of teleological thinking are known as egoism, act-utilitarianism, and rule-utilitarianism. Each approach has its defenders, although some form of utilitarianism is most prevalent among ethical relativists.

Egoism takes the position that everyone should promote his own self-interest, because then the greatest good will accrue to the greatest number. We are taught not to be self-serving, but it may be said that all codes of behavior, laws, etc., have the basic foundation of rational self-interest, even though it may also serve to benefit the group or society and other individuals, as well.

Pojman (2002) describes what may be the least unacceptable form of egoism, calling it universal ethical egoism. Among its supporters are Adam Smith, Ayn Rand, and Thomas Hobbes. The basic premise is "that everyone ought to do what will maximize one's own expected utility or bring about one's own happiness, even when it means harming others. This is not considered egotistical; rather, it is seen as prudential, favoring long-term interests over short-term interests. In its most sophisticated form universal ethical egoism urges everyone to *try* to win in the game of life, and it recognizes that in order to do this, some compromises are necessary. Indeed, the universal egoist will admit that to some extent we must all give up a certain freedom and cooperate with others to achieve our ends" (90).

Economists who follow the lead of Adam Smith maintain "that individual self-interest in a competitive marketplace produces a state of optimal goodness for society at large, because the peculiar nature of self-interested competition causes each individual to produce a better product and sell it at a lower price than competitors. Thus, enlightened self-interest leads, as if by an invisible hand, to the best overall situation" (Pojman 2002, 91).

Ayn Rand argues that finding happiness is the goal of life, and altruism requires that we sacrifice our happiness for the good of others, which is contrary to our highest good. Therefore, in order to reach "the perfection of one's abilities in a state of happiness . . . [and thereby reach] the highest goal for humans . . . we [must] seek our own happiness exclusively" (Pojman 2002, 91–92).

Hobbes takes what is called the *psychological egoist* approach, although not in its purist sense. This approach argues that we have a strong psychological urge to pursue our own interests, and "since we cannot do otherwise without unreasonable effort, it follows that it is morally permissible to act entirely out of self-interest." However, in order to achieve long-term egoist goals, we must avoid doing those things that would inhibit our reaching them. Therefore, we may even follow the Golden Rule if it will help ensure that others do good to us (Pojman 2002, 92).

Most of us find little attraction in egoism as an ethical practice, probably because it is so contrary to most social norms, even though in our more honest moments we may admit to following its precepts at times. It tends to exclude many of the deepest human values such as love and friendship while also violating principles of fairness and humane service to others.

Utilitarianism emphasizes two main features from relativism: (1) The **consequentialist principle**, which states "that the rightness or wrongness of an act is determined by the goodness or badness of the results that flow from it. It is the end, not the means, that counts; the end justifies the means" (Pojman 2002, 109); and (2) The **utility principle,** which "views pleasure as the sole good and pain as the only evil. An act is right if it either brings about more pleasure than pain or prevents pain, and an act is wrong if it either brings about more pain than pleasure or prevents pleasure from occurring" (109). Mill went on to define pleasure or happiness in terms of certain types of higher order pleasures or satisfactions, such as intellectual, aesthetic, and social enjoyments, as well as in terms of minimal suffering. He argues that the higher, or more refined, pleasures are superior to the lower ones.

Act-utilitarianism is one of the two classical types of utilitarianism, the other being rule-utilitarianism. It proposes that "an act is right if and only if it results in as much good as any available alternative" (Pojman 2002, 111). Mill stated the principle as "actions are right in proportion as they tend to promote happiness, wrong as they tend to produce the reverse of happiness" (Piest 1957, 10). Both definitions illustrate the concept of defining right action according to the best perception and wisdom of the agent at the moment. We may rely on "rule of thumb" for practical purposes and in order to be able to act as quickly as necessary, but the right act is still the one expected by the individual to result in the most utility.

At first glance, act-utilitarianism seems plausible, although somewhat clumsy in use and subject to individual errors in perception or judgment.

However, further observation reveals that it seems contrary to fundamental in-tuitions about correct behavior. Richard Brandt's criticism is a good illustration of this problem.

> It implies that if you have employed a boy to mow your lawn and he has finished the job and asks for his pay, you should pay him what you promised only if you can not find a better use for your money. It implies that when you bring home your monthly paycheck you should use it to support your family and yourself only if it cannot be used more effectively to supply the needs of others. It implies that if your father is ill and has no prospect of good in his life, and maintaining him is a drain on the energy and enjoyments of others, then, if you can end his life without provoking any public scandal or setting a bad example, it is your positive duty to take matters into your own hands and bring his life to a close (from S. Gorovitz, Ed. 1971, 109–110).

Mill counters this argument to some extent by making the point "that even when a person's conduct is motivated by the principle of the 'general good,' this does not mean that he must think of the whole human race. He need not think of anyone beyond the particular persons involved in the situation in which he is acting, of their good and their happiness, first making sure, how-ever, that no one else will thereby be harmed" (Adler and Cain 1962, 264).

Mill admits that an individual's actions are rightly guided by the feelings and customs of society and that this contributes to individual happiness. Therefore, actions are to some extent, at least, determined by social custom and accepted practice, regardless of effects on an individual's personal happiness. It is also logical that our actions should be guided by the experience of the ages and general agreement about what is useful and good (264). Lying, killing, or stealing thus would not be considered an acceptable course of action, regardless of the good resulting for the individual. However, "Mill admits exceptions to . . . transcendent obligations . . . for the sake of a greater utility. One may lie, or commit other acts generally considered harmful, to prevent a greater harm in a particular case. . . . The guiding principle, however, the ultimate criterion, is still utility or expediency" (265–266). The objective result of an action, not the motivation behind the action, makes the ethical difference. However, the stan-dard is not the agent's own greatest happiness, but the "greatest amount of hap-piness altogether" (Adler and Cain 1962, 262).

Rule-utilitarianism tries to avoid the major criticisms of act-utilitarian-ism while keeping the tenets of relativism. It is somewhat related to deontology, in that rules are developed by which actions are guided, but these rules are de-veloped according to their utility, their probability of producing the best results for the most people, rather than according to divine law or natural law.

Instead of saying, as do the act-utilitarians, that "everyone should always *act* to bring about the greatest good for all concerned," rule-utilitarians propose that "everyone should always establish and follow that rule or those rules that will bring about the greatest good for all concerned. Rule utilitarians try, from experience and careful reasoning, to set up a series of rules that, when followed, will yield the greatest good for all humanity" (Thiroux 1998, 45, 46). These moral codes are not universal, however, for they are appropriate only for a single society and certain kinds of situations. They are not "good" intrinsically, but rather are judged "good" because following such rules would result in the greatest overall aggregate utility.

Denhardt (1988) further describes rule-utilitarianism as an approach that

> . . . accepts the notion that certain moral principles can be derived from experience and can form a type of moral code to be followed by members of a society. However, the moral principles are not universal (for they are appropriate for a single society at a given point in time), and they are not "good" intrinsically, but rather are judged "good" because following such rules would result in the greatest overall aggregate utility. Thus, rule utilitarianism differs from act utilitarianism in that some generalizable rules of conduct can be established. But these rules of conduct are different from the deontological approach (52).

Brandt further explains that "an act is right if and only if it would not be prohibited by the moral code ideal for the society" (Gorovitz 1971, 331).

The rule-utilitarian approach tries to escape some of the more serious conflicts between act-utilitarianism and common moral beliefs and "intuitions." Examples may be rather easily found where an act-utilitarian would say that in individual cases it is not wrong to kill innocent people, to invade their rights, to torture opponents, to break solemn agreements, to cheat, or to betray a trust, if by so doing a "greater utility" might be obtained. But the rule-utilitarian would say that such individual acts would be wrong, because if these kinds of acts were generally acceptable it would have a very bad effect on the general happiness. Rule-utilitarians would probably agree that it is right to lie in order to save an innocent life or to protect those who might be subject to unfair and cruel treatment because of political, religious, or racial conflicts (lying to protect Anne Frank). Murder or genocide would not be acceptable, but perhaps capital punishment or dropping of the atomic bomb on Hiroshima would be.

Arguments for and against Relativism and Teleology

Arguments in favor of relativism and teleology may begin with Mill's contention that all people desire and seek happiness, which is, therefore, an end in itself. All human actions are, and should be, attempts to achieve the end of happiness or well being, and one person deserves happiness just as much as another.

Others who favor relativism stress that "it just makes sense." Even in the "hard" sciences, relativity is accepted. In addition, our sense of justice gives it support, as do the various and profound changes occurring in the world today. Most legislation these days is crafted with a utilitarian test in mind. In addition, relativism promotes tolerance, without accepting the notion that "anything goes."

Other arguments in favor of the form of teleology we call utilitarianism are related to the disadvantages identified with objectivity and deontology. It helps us avoid blindly following rules when they are no longer appropriate, when our intuition tells us that they are wrong in particular situations, or when they fail to make accommodations for social change and technological development. Rule-utilitarianism, in particular, gives us a criterion for doing the "good"—achieving general happiness. Reform of unfair laws or rules is not only acceptable, but desirable.

Egalitarian concepts (often called fairness or justice) are argued to favor relativism, the basic idea being that "good people should fare well and bad people should fare badly." Among other things, egalitarianism argues that similar cases should be treated similarly and different cases differently. This outlaws discrimination on the basis of race, sex, etc., because it causes dissimilar treatment of relevantly similar cases.

Egalitarianism also maintains that innocent people should not suffer through no fault of their own, and exploitation—taking unfair advantage of an innocent person's situation—is wrong. People should not profit from their own wrongdoing and the punishment should fit the crime (be proportional). Promises should be kept, merit should be rewarded, reciprocity and gratitude are important. All of these premises of egalitarianism require at times the exercise of principles from the theory of relativism (Harwood, from L. P. Pojman, Ed. 1993, 24).

Perhaps the strongest argument for utilitarianism is it provides a way to logically decide which rule should prevail when one basic principle comes into conflict with another (justice and duty, for example).

Arguments against relativism, teleology, and utilitarianism include those that are related to perceived advantages of objectivism and deontology. They bring up philosophical objections to equating "is" with "ought," as utility becomes confused with justice and fact becomes confused with value (Haynes 1998, 104). Defining what is "good" may become a matter of opinion or majority rule when there seem to be a variety of goods and reasonable, ethical people may disagree as to their relative value. "Utilitarianism cannot identify *one* good that is both necessary and sufficient for human flourishing. Human flourishing seems to be marked by a variety of goods, and reasonable, ethical people may well disagree in their assessment of which goods are most important" (Ottensmeyer and McCarthy 1996, 11).

Other opponents maintain that we need specific and strong guides for behavior in a world that is basically evil, that without specific and stable principles and rules we have no way of determining who will decide what is right and wrong—and on what basis. When groups differ in their beliefs about what should and should not be done, which group's preferences will be judged right and what will be the rational basis for such a judgement? Those who disagree with relativism maintain that God didn't give us "ten suggestions," because He knew that we need direction.

Opponents of relativism also point out that if happiness for the greatest number becomes the guideline, then the majority opinion will prevail, creating intolerance and dismissing social reformers, minorities, and dissidents as hopelessly wrong. It is argued that relativism cannot rationally specify which group's beliefs determine right and wrong, and if we rely on the majority then relativism will be too intolerant, since it will not accept moral reformers, minorities, and dissidents. We need to go beyond what philosophers call *conventional morality* (the prevailing notion about what is best) to *critical morality* (what is really best) (Harwood 1996, 2–4). Everything that is good will bring some person or group happiness, but it does not follow that everything that brings someone happiness is necessarily good.

Some who oppose relativism do so with the argument that it does not give enough value to promise keeping and truth telling. This argument points out that civilized society will soon flounder if insufficient value is given to these two standards, and trying to establish principles by which they may be violated is very difficult, if not impossible.

Another argument against relativism has to do with how to establish the reasonable limits of what should be done to create the "greatest happiness for the greatest number." If it is acceptable for airplane crash victims trapped in the mountains to survive by eating a companion who has died, should this idea be carried to the point of saying it would be acceptable for the least useful person of the group who is still alive to be killed and eaten to keep the rest of the group alive? "Utilitarianism demands too much . . . that our actions aim at producing the greatest likely net good. Not only must we avoid harming people, we are duty-bound to help them, putting the interests of all parties on a par with our own" (Ottensmeyer and McCarthy 1996, 12). If it is good for a person to give one kidney to keep another person alive, would it be even better to sacrifice oneself so as to donate all of your organs and thus keep several people alive? Should a well-off person or country give of their goods to the point of poverty in order to help the poor of the world? Should one whose favorite form of recreation is golf sell his golf clubs and give the money to an organization that will use the money to buy medical supplies for emergencies?

A practical difficulty has to do with the fact that it is very difficult, if not impossible, to determine all the consequences of an action in advance, let alone evaluate their relative value. Another practical consideration involves the concern that "insistence on choosing impartially a course of action that will maximize net good for everyone involved overlooks the fact that at times decision-makers have special ties and responsibilities to certain people" (Ottensmeyer and McCarthy 1996, 12).

Additionally, as pointed out by Mackie (1977), it can be argued that "the denial of objective values can carry with it an extreme emotional reaction, a feeling that nothing matters at all, that life has lost its purpose" (34). If this happens, the individuals or groups are likely to lose all sense of direction, resulting in loss of motivation and little if any significant accomplishment. While teleologists argue that differences in established rules of conduct over time prove that there is no universal moral order, "the deontologists would argue that the moral order exists but is not yet fully understood" (Denhardt 1988, 45).

Case Studies

A Reference Request

As principal of Normal High School, John Checkers had escaped most of the really serious problems that he heard about from his colleagues around the state. Unfortunately, he was now faced with a situation that taxed his professional skill and wisdom. Rolly Durham was a well-liked and successful English teacher who had been at Normal for all ten years that John had been principal. In fact, they came to the school in the same year—and they were about the same age. Their association had been closer than is usually the case between a principal and a teacher, and they shared membership in the same service club. Perhaps that is why Rolly felt he could ask for some special help.

Rolly recently confided to John that he tested HIV-positive about four years ago, evidently having been infected through a blood transfusion received during surgery many years earlier. He had just recently been diagnosed with full-blown AIDS. Rolly went on to say that he wanted to move to a large city about 200 miles away where he could receive the latest treatment while continuing to teach. Teaching was his passion, and without the income and the other rewards of teaching, he wasn't sure he could maintain an attitude that would help him cope with the disease. Besides, he felt that he still had a lot to offer young people and would continue to help as many as possible for as long as possible.

The part of the situation that perplexed John had to do with the fact that Rolly was a finalist for a department chair teaching position in the city where good treatment was available for AIDS patients, and he needed a good recommendation from his principal. He had been told by the principal who interviewed him that he was impressed with Rolly's having been in the same school for his entire teaching career, because he was looking for someone to give stability and long-term leadership in the school. Rolly had given John's name as a reference, and the principal of the school where he was an applicant had called earlier in the day. Another complicating factor was that the principal of the school considering employing Rolly was a good professional friend, as he and John had been involved together in the activities of the state principals' association on several occasions.

As he mentally debated the situation, John reached for the telephone. He wasn't sure what he should say to his professional colleague at the other school, especially if he were asked about Rolly's health or whether he would be likely to stay in the new position for an extended period of time.

Questions to Consider

1. If one believes that telling the truth is an important ethical principle, what options does John have in this case?
2. Are there ethical principles in this case that conflict with that of "truthtelling"? If so, which should receive priority?
3. Which aspects of this case would be considered more important to one who subscribes to ethical relativism as opposed to one who subscribes to ethical objectivism?
4. How might John approach this if he believes in trying to balance objectivist ethical principles with consideration of consequences?
5. Are there other options that John should advise Rolly to consider?
6. How will John justify his actions to Rolly if the position is denied Rolly because of information that John gives the other principal?

Dangerous, Or Just Immature?

Things just haven't been the same in the office of principal John Upjohn since the implementation of the zero tolerance policy at the beginning of the school year at Normal Middle School. Located in a rural community, most serious discipline problems occurred rarely and John had enjoyed the flexibility to be somewhat tolerant of his hormone-challenged charges. After all, this is a middle school, and the students here are just as unpredictable as anywhere else.

This was again apparent this morning when seventh grader Jackie Smart was caught with a small pocketknife in his jeans pocket by Mr. Stern, the no-nonsense math teacher. Mr. Upjohn knows that the new policy is very specific, requiring that anyone caught with a knife be sent to the county alternative school for three weeks. Little Jackie would certainly have his problems there. The new policy was initiated at the insistence of the school board president, who is known far and wide as a "law and order" man and currently also serves as president of the local chapter of the National Rifle Association. Mr. Upjohn also knows that Jackie, who lives in poverty with his disabled grandmother, wouldn't and couldn't hurt a flea. The deck always seems to be stacked against Jackie.

As far as Mr. Upjohn is concerned, no harm has been done. The boy just enjoyed carrying his late father's old pocketknife while he was at home, and he forgot to take it out of his pocket this morning. Surely it would be all right to give Jackie a good lecture and send him back to class. After all, even the football coach (and he's tough!) gives his boys a second chance (Contributed by Bobbie Eddins).

Questions to Consider

1. How does the ethical theory of relativism, particularly utilitarianism, fit into the new zero tolerance policy at Normal Middle School? Would

this policy be viewed with approval by an absolutist, as described in Chapter 3?

2. Does Mr. Upjohn have any choice in this case relative to Jackie's punishment?

3. Should the alternative school have arrangements for treating students differently according to their misbehavior?

4. Could some special training for teachers after the new policy was initiated have helped avoid this kind of problem? If so, what should it include?

5. What effect do zero tolerance policies have relative to punishment for more severe misbehavior? What can be done to "make the punishment fit the crime" when there is more serious misbehavior under this type of policy?

Activities and Discussion Questions

1. Does act-utilitarianism or rule-utilitarianism best fit the needs of a middle school principal in dealing with student discipline?

2. If your school board demands a zero tolerance policy, how might you try to influence thinking relative to its application?

3. Describe a dilemma that your school community is facing. Ask three community leaders who are not directly involved to suggest (a) their best thinking about developing a solution to the dilemma, and (b) the principles they used to decide what their suggestion should be. Compare their solutions and their guiding principles.

4. Consider the decision you recently made as an educational leader. Characterize your thought process as you made the decision in terms of utility versus justice. In making your decision, did you rely more on fact or opinion?

5. Make a chart, showing on one side arguments in favor of utilitarianism and on the other side arguments against it. If you favor some form of utilitarianism, does act-utilitarianism or rule-utilitarianism seem best in light of these arguments? Why?

6. What seem to be the strongest forces determining generally held concepts of right and wrong in our society? Are minorities adequately represented in these determinations?

7. Find a rule in a student code of conduct that was probably not there ten years ago. Explain why the rule is there now. Then identify a former rule that is not in the code today. Why was it removed?

8. If one values the need for utility, what rules or practices in your school may need revising due to changes in social expectations and acceptance?

9. Identify some situations or rules in our schools where punishment is predetermined, regardless of the consequences.

References

Abelson, R. and Friquegnon, M. (1975). *Ethics for modern life.* New York: St. Martin's Press.

Adler, M. and Cain, S. (1962). *Ethics: The study of moral values.* Chicago: Encyclopedia Britannica.

Denhardt, K. G. (1988). *The ethics of public service.* Westport, CO: Greenwood Press.

Gorovitz, S., ed. (1971). *Mill: Utilitarianism with critical essays.* Indianapolis: Bobbs-Merrill.

Hare, R. M. (1952). "The language of morals." In R. Abelson and M. Friquegnon, 1975. *Ethics for modern life.* New York: St. Martin's Press.

Harwood, S. (1996). *Business as ethical and business as usual.* Sudbury, MA: Jones and Bartlett Publishers

Haynes, F. (1998). *The ethical school.* New York: Routledge.

The Holy Bible, New International Version. International Bible Society, 1973.

Kidder, R. M. (1995). *How good people make tough choices.* New York: William Morrow and Company.

Mackie, J. L. (1977). *Ethics: Inventing right and wrong.* New York: Penguin Books.

MacIntyre, A. (1966). *A short history of ethics.* New York: Macmillan.

Moore, G. E. (1949). Principia ethica. In R. Abelson and M. Friquegnon, 1975. *Ethics for modern life.* New York: St. Martin's Press.

Ottensmeyer, E. J. and McCarthy, G. D. (1996). *Ethics in the workplace.* New York: McGraw-Hill.

Piest, O., ed. (1957). *Utilitarianism.* New York: Bobbs-Merrill.

Pojman, L. P., ed. (1993). *Moral philosophy: A reader.* Indianapolis: Hackett Publishing.

Pojman, L. P. (2002). *Ethics: Discovering right and wrong,* (4th ed.). Belmont, CA: Wadsworth.

Thiroux, J. (1998). *Ethics: Theory and practice,* (6th ed.). Upper Saddle River, NJ: Prentice Hall.

5

Axiology (Value Theory) and Motive (Character)

Ethical Theory: Axiology (Value)

In the introductory chapter to this book, it was stated that one of the book's major purposes is to help educational administrators know how to deal with *dilemmas*, those situations in which none of the choices available for action seem quite right, or they all seem to have some negative aspects. At this point in our study of ethics, we seem to be facing a dilemma relative to choosing an ethical theory and a guide to follow to make decisions and take actions. Objectivism, with its rules, and relativism, with its primary attention to consequences, both seem to be desirable in some ways and undesirable in some ways. Is there a way to incorporate what we consider the positives of each theory into something that will avoid what seem to be the negatives of each? Some who grapple with this question consider the concept of value theory (from axiology, the study of values) and character (as judged by motive) to be the best solution to this problem.

Value theory identifies "virtues" as the key to ethical thought and action, first pointing out that one must not confuse virtue with values. *Values* is a morally neutral term indicating preference, while *virtue* is "a quality of character by which individuals habitually recognize and *do* the right thing" (Woodward 1995, 208).

Value theory incorporates some of the basic ideas from both objectivism and relativity, and it may help you to understand the "big picture" of how to best approach ethics in educational leadership. Value ethics tries to describe the good or virtuous person and show how such a person may be developed. This contrasts with the objectivist's attempts to identify good rules or acts that are to be followed without much thought or question. It also contrasts with the relativist who tries to achieve good consequences. Some additional terminology is used in this effort, and traditional terminology is used in different ways at times. This can become confusing, but we will now investigate how this third way to approach ethical thinking is described and applied by those who advocate its use, beginning with Socrates and Aristotle.

Axiology and Value Theory. Philosophers, from Socrates to the present, begin their deliberations with a question—"What makes life worth living?" or "What is the good life?" This question is the genesis of axiology (the study of good and bad, right and wrong) and the value system that develops from a person's definition of the good life. Most of us develop a value system without really thinking about it, following the lead provided by parents, teachers, and the society of which we are a part. Such an "inherited" group of values (they don't really constitute a "system" unless we are more direct and thoughtful in developing them) may serve most people adequately as they move through life. But for those in leadership positions and others who are faced with difficult choices, something more cohesive and rational is needed. Particularly when faced with dilemmas, a value system is required that will help us arrive at the best decision and course of action.

Perhaps we should have started this discussion of value theory before getting into definitions of important concepts and questions about objectivity and subjectivity, but it is by now probably more obvious that a study of axiology and values is needed. There should be a better awareness of difficulties related to understanding and taking action according to "good and bad," "right and wrong," and sources of values.

Historical Development and Basic Principles. To answer the question "What is the good life?" and decide what things or activities are valuable, one must first define what is meant by the word "good." Is what is good for one person necessarily good for another? If not, which good is superior? What values form the foundation or starting point for defining good? What kinds of things are either good or bad? Do we confuse "good" with "preferred"? And just how strong is our commitment to values circumscribed by our definition of "good"?

Socrates identified three kinds of good:

1. The purely intrinsic (simple joys of health, love, nature, and beauty, for example; with disvalues of pain, suffering and loneliness).
2. The purely instrumental goods (such as medicine and making money), which allow other "goods" to be achieved.
3. Combinations (such as knowledge, sight, and health,) which are good in themselves and good as a means to further goods. (Pojman 2002, 63–64).

Will Durant (1953), a popular philosopher among "nonphilosophers," pointed out that Aristotle set the direction for future philosophers when he recognized the "question of questions—what is the best life?—what is life's supreme good?—what is virtue?—how shall we find happiness and fulfillment?" He defined "good" by concluding that "the aim of life is not goodness for its own sake, but happiness. 'For we choose happiness for itself, and never with a view to anything further; whereas we choose honor, pleasure, intellect . . . because we believe that through them we shall be made happy'" (60).

Virtue, then, becomes that which produces happiness, but not in the shallow sense so often used today. The true meaning of happiness comes back to that which culminates in a good life, a life which is worthwhile. So happiness develops a depth far beyond the superficial pleasures with which the word is usually associated.

According to Aristotle, the ultimate goal of life is *eudaimonea*. This Greek word is usually interpreted in English as "happiness." However, this interpretation is not really adequate. As explained by Thomson and Missner (2000), the Greek word is more akin to the concept of "flourishing." It occurs "when someone is using all of their powers to their fullest extent, and things are going as well as they could" (68).

The good life, as described by Aristotle, "is one that will result in happiness and that will involve matters of chance, but also some matters that are under our own control. We should endeavor to have a life that engages our capacities to reason and to see what is involved in developing excellent traits of character, because character traits contribute more to happiness than any other factor that we can control" (Thomson and Missner 2000, 83).

Once we have reached a satisfactory understanding of what we mean by the good life and happiness, values (the building blocks of virtue) become desirable for the purpose of creating or maintaining happiness. As summarized by Mackie (1977), Aristotle emphasizes the importance of values or virtues and how they are developed by stating that "each virtue is a disposition for making (right) choices, and one that is trained or developed by experience rather than inborn" (186). Through training and experience, the virtuous person may learn best to make the right choices (choose values) by finding a "middle way."

In his work on ethics, *Nicomachean Ethics*, Aristotle describes the virtuous person as one with ". . . the state of character which makes a man good and which makes him do his own work well" (Hutchins 1952, 351). He goes on to say that "it is possible to fail in many ways . . . while to succeed is possible only in one way. . . ; for these reasons . . . then, excess and defect are characteristic of vice, and the mean of virtue; for men are good in but one way, but bad in many" and "virtue is a kind of mean, since . . . it aims at what is intermediate" (352). This statement and the discussion accompanying it led to what is called the **golden mean**. A virtue can thus be identified as that desirable point between the two extremes of excess or deficit (the "just right" point between too much and too little). A vice is at one or the other of the extremes, a virtue somewhere in between. But there are also obvious vices that have no mean. As Aristotle phrased it:

> Virtue, then, is a state of character concerned with choice, lying in a mean, i.e. the mean relative to us, this being determined by a rational principle, and by that principle by which the man of practical wisdom would determine it. Now it is a mean between two vices, that which depends on excess and that which depends on defect; and again it is a mean because the vices respectively fall short of or exceed what is right in both passions and actions, while virtue both finds and chooses that which is intermediate.
>
> But not every action nor every passion admits of a mean; for some have names that already imply badness, e.g. spite, shamelessness, envy, and in the case of actions adultery, theft, murder; for all of these and such-like things imply by their names that they are themselves bad, and not the excesses or deficiencies of them. It is not possible, then, ever to be right with regard to them; one must always be wrong (Hutchins 1952, 352).
>
> With regard to honour and dishonour the mean is proper pride, the excess is known as a sort of "empty vanity," and the deficiency is undue humility; and as we said liberality was related to magnificence, differing from it by dealing with small sums, so there is a state similarly related to proper pride, being concerned with small honours while that is concerned with great . . .the intermediate state is in all things to be praised, but . . . we must incline sometimes towards the excess, sometimes toward the deficiency; for so shall we most easily hit the mean and what is right (Hutchins 1952, 353, 355).

The golden mean is not, like the mathematical mean, an exact midpoint between two precisely calculable extremes. It moves between the extremes, depending on the circumstances of each situation as determined through reason and experience, by training and habit.

For instance, fear and confidence, anger and pity, and pleasure and pain may be felt both too much and too little, and in either case not well; but to feel them at the right times, with reference to the right objects, toward the right people, with the right motive, and in the right way is what is both intermediate and best, and this is characteristic of virtue (Aristotle, in Hutchins, ed. 1952, 352).

But how does one determine what is right? There seem to be few if any rules, and consequences are not used by Aristotle as a way to determine the "rightness" of actions. Virtuous action (excellence) is seen as an art rather than a science, exemplified as a characteristic attitude. "Plato had [this] in mind when he called virtue harmonious action; Socrates when he identified virtue with knowledge" (Durant 1953, 61).

The choice of the "mean," then, becomes of utmost importance. So how does one go about making the best choice? Aristotle says that it "depends on 'the right rule,' which is determined through the intellectual virtue of prudence or practical wisdom" (Adler and Cain 1962, 58). He proposes that these are developed through education, following the example of other virtuous persons, and through experience.

As indicated in the discussion above, much of what is considered helpful relative to virtue and values we owe to the Greeks, even though some have changed the definition and equated virtue with certain customs or rules. Value theory in the prevailing definition still relies on the basic thinking passed to us by Aristotle, although Christianity and other religions provide some significant principles relative to how one finds the golden mean. Those who subscribe to this approach to ethics simply face the challenge of placing the golden mean at the right spot in each situation (no small task in many situations, of course).

Value theory is used by both objectivists and relativists at times to support their case. The objectivist identifies principles to guide action, those principles seen to be the golden mean, while the relativists like to use the concept of happiness (defined in some utilitarian fashion) to support their case. The objectivist identifies the "right," while the relativist identifies the "good."

Writing for educational leaders, Hodgkinson (1991) gives a more modern view as he identifies the "right" and the "good" as two models of the value concept. He draws the typical distinction between the axiological (good) and the deontological (right). Good refers to what is enjoyable, likable, pleasurable; right to what is proper, moral, what ought to be. "Good is known directly as a matter of preference. The knowledge of good comes spontaneously from impulse or direct introspection . . . It may be innate, biochemical, genetic, or else learned, programmed, conditioned. It is part of our biological make-up and is essentially hedonistic, summed up in the elemental psychology of seeking pleasure and avoiding pain." The "right" is determined by a moral sense, or sense of collective responsibility, a conscience" (98).

In discussing how we may go about validating and justifying given concepts of the desirable in various contexts, Hodgkinson goes on to identify three types of value (100–101):

Type III values are self-justifying and rooted in a person's emotional structure. These are identified above as the "good."

Type II values are considered "right," either on the basis of consequences or consensus. Rooted in reason and logic, these values are collective and social.

Type I values are grounded in principle, supported by the metaphysical. They take the form of ethical codes, injunctions or commandments. They do not rely on either science or logic and require invoking the will to produce an act of faith or commitment. In addition, there are *metavalues*, which are concepts "of the desirable so vested and entrenched that it seems to be beyond dispute or contention" (110).

Another approach to developing skill in ethical decision making is similar to those described above but with a somewhat different emphasis as a "third way." Kidder (1995) uses the terms *rules-based thinking* in referring to objectivism/deontology and *ends-based thinking* to identify relativism/teleology. A third way of thinking about ethics he calls *care-based thinking*. Others have used the phrase *ethics of caring* in similar fashion. This approach puts love for others first and is exemplified in the Golden Rule: "Do to others what you would like them to do to you"; or put yourself in another's shoes. Often associated with Christianity, this concept is prevalent in most of the world's great religions (24–25).

Nel Noddings (1995) is perhaps the best known advocate of caring as an ethical foundation. Coming from what she sees as a more typically feminine approach to ethics, she argues this concept as follows:

> Ethical argumentation has frequently proceeded as if it were governed by the logical necessity characteristic of geometry. It has concentrated on the establishment of principles and that which can be logically derived from them. One might say that ethics has been discussed largely in the language of the father: in principles and propositions, in terms such as justification, fairness, justice. The mother's voice has been silent. Human caring and the memory of caring and being cared for, which I shall argue form the foundation of ethical response have not received attention except as outcomes of ethical behavior. One is tempted to say that ethics has so far been guided by Logos, the masculine spirit, whereas the more natural and, perhaps stronger approach would be through Eros, the feminine spirit. . . building an ethic on caring . . . is not . . . that form of act-utilitarianism commonly labeled "situation ethics." Its emphasis is not on the consequences of our acts, although these are not, of course, irrelevant. But an ethic of caring locates morality primarily in the pre-act consciousness of the one-caring (38, 40).

How are we to make judgments of right and wrong under this "ethic of caring"? Noddings explains further.

> The caring attitude that lies at the heart of all ethical behavior is universal. . . In general the one-caring evaluates her own acts with respect to how faithfully they conform to what is known and felt through the receptivity of caring. But she also uses "right" and "wrong" instructively and respectfully to refer to the judgments of significant others. If she agrees because the matter at hand can be assessed in light of caring, she adds her personal commitment and example; if she has doubts—because the rule appealed to seems irrelevant or ambiguous in the light of caring—she still acknowledges the judgment but adds her own dissent or demurrer. Her eye is on the ethical development of the cared-for and, as she herself withholds judgment until she has heard the "whole story," she wants the cared-for to encounter others, receive them, and reflect on what he has received. Principles and rules are among the beliefs he will receive, and she wants him to consider these in the light of caring.
>
> Caring preserves both the group and the individual and . . . it limits our obligation so that it may realistically be met. It will not allow us to be

distracted by visions of universal love, perfect justice, or a world unified under principle. It does not say, "Thou shalt not kill," and then seek other principles under which killing is, after all, justified. If the other is a clear and immediate danger to me or to my cared-fors, I must stop him, and I might need to kill him. But I cannot kill in the name of principle or justice (42–43, 45).

Action Guide: Motive (Character)

We have discussed both positives and negatives of value theory. How well does it seem to work as an actual guide to ethical decision making? The determining factor as to whether a person is virtuous is their motive for action, which is governed by what we call character. Rather than judging an action as ethical primarily by whether it follows some rule or principle or according to the consequences that may follow, value theory leads to identifying an action as ethical or unethical according to the motive of the agent.

If a good character (one embodying essential virtues) is the basis for virtuous action, then we should proceed to describe it. What are the character traits (virtues) found in a virtuous person? Woodward (1995) provides an overview of those character traits considered "virtuous."

Aristotle and many others advocated four "classical" virtues. Generally considered just as compelling today as in Aristotle's day, they are prudence, justice, fortitude, and temperance. Prudence is the practical ability to recognize and make the right choice in specific situations. Justice includes fairness, honesty and promise keeping. Fortitude is the courage to take the right action in the most difficult of circumstances. Temperance, involving much more than alcoholic drink, is self-discipline to control all the human passions and sensual pleasures.

Beyond the four "classical" virtues above, different societies emphasize different virtues and add new ones. Loyalty is often added, and obedience to God's commands was primary to ancient Israel. Christianity added four theological virtues—faith, hope, charity, and humility. Others virtues, such as compassion, are often added to the list (208–209).

Martin and Jones, as cited in Harwood (1966, 26), include examples of how the golden mean lies between the vices of excess and deficit. Combined and clarified for this text, they include the following.

Situation	Excess	Mean	Deficit
Fear	foolhardiness	courage	cowardice
Giving gifts	extravagance	generosity	miserliness
Self-appraisal	vanity	proper pride	inferiority
Response to insults	anger	patience	apathy
Social conduct	obsequiousness	friendliness	rudeness/sulkiness

Physical appetites	overindulgence	temperance	overly inhibited
Personal flaws awareness	shyness	modesty	shamelessness
Claiming honors	vanity	pride	humility
Self-expression	boastfulness	truthfulness	false modesty
Conversation/humor	buffoonery	wittiness	boorishness

Harwood shortens the above to list the following as "the main character traits that are virtues (forms of excellence tending to constitute a good character), or vices (character flaws tending to constitute a bad character):

1. Courage is a virtue and cowardice is a vice.
2. Honesty is a virtue and dishonesty is a vice.
3. Kindness is a virtue and unkindness is a vice.
4. Loyalty is a virtue and disloyalty is a vice.
5. Gratitude is a virtue and ingratitude is a vice.
6. Charity is a virtue and uncharitableness is a vice.
7. Being forgiving exhibits a virtue and being unforgiving exhibits a vice" (25).

Others would add additional character traits as attributes of a virtuous person, such as cleanliness and silence (Franklin), caring (Kidder, Noddings and others), and humility (Jesus).

Character, then, is the ability to make the best decision when a decision is required. This best decision may be according to a basic virtue which allows of no variation, or it may be the golden mean between two extremes, described as "the perfect thing for a particular person to do in a particular situation" (Thomson and Missner 2000, 79).

But how does one acquire good character and gain the ability to make the best decision in each situation? Aristotle thinks that the best way to develop a skill is not by following rules or steps, but by proceeding as one would develop any skill—more a matter of practice and observation. "The best that we can do is to work on our virtues, develop our characters, and then we will be able to judge and perceive what should be done. This is the best that can be done" (Thomson and Missner 2000, 84).

Are there guidelines to help us know if we are making progress in our efforts to make good decisions in difficult situations? Kohlberg (1984) suggests that those who desire to improve their ability to apply moral virtues may monitor their progress by using a system that identifies six stages of moral judgment divided into three levels. Level 1 (the preconventional level) includes Stage 1 and Stage 2. A person acting at the Stage 1 level obeys rules because of fear of punishment and the superior power of authorities. An egocentric point of view results in failure to consider the interests of others or recognize that they differ from the actor's. Obedience is valued for its own sake, and actions are considered physically rather in terms of other's psychological interests (174).

Stage 2 involves following rules only when it is to someone's immediate interest (your own or others). Because everybody has his own interest to pursue, right is relative according to concrete, individualistic needs. One must recognize other people's needs and reconcile them with one's own (174).

Level II (the conventional level) includes Stages 3 and 4. A person at Stage 3 of moral judgment has a need to be seen as a good person, living up to what is expected by others and by one's own belief system. It involves keeping mutual relationships, such as trust, loyalty, respect, and gratitude. Belief in the Golden Rule results in a desire to maintain rules and authority that support stereotypically good behavior. Kohlberg puts most adults at this stage of moral development (174).

Stage 4 of moral judgment adds consideration of the social system. Laws are to be upheld except in extreme cases where they conflict with other fixed social duties. Right action is that which contributes to society, the group, or the institution. One must fulfill defined obligations in the social system, living in a way that would maintain the desired social system if everyone acted in the same way. Individual relations are defined according to how they fit into the social system (175).

Level III (the postconventional or principled level) includes Stages 5 and 6. Stage 5 follows concepts of social contract, utility and individual rights. Recognizing that people hold a variety of values and opinions, and that most values and rules vary from group to group, a person at this stage of moral judgment still supports those values and rules that are accepted by a group. They should be upheld in the interest of impartiality and because they are part of a "social contract." There are some nonrelative values and rights, however, like life and liberty, which must be upheld in any society and regardless of majority opinion. There is a sense of obligation to law because of the social contract to make and abide by laws for the welfare of all and for the protection of all people's rights. There is also concern that laws and duties should be based on rational calculation of overall utility, the "greatest good for the greatest number." There is recognition that moral and legal standards sometimes conflict, creating difficulty in integrating them. Kohlberg estimated that 20 to 25 percent of adults fall into this stage of moral development (175).

Stage 6 includes those who follow self-chosen ethical principles. Particular laws or social agreements are usually valid because they rest on such principles, but when laws violate these principles, a person must act in accordance with the accepted principle. "Principles are universal principles of justice; the equality of human rights and respect for the dignity of human beings as individual persons." There is a belief in and commitment to the validity of universal moral principles, developed rationally and following the perspective that persons are ends in themselves and must be treated as such. Kohlberg estimated that only 5–10 percent of adults operate at this level of moral judgment (176).

Closely related to the "ethics of care" described above, an approach commonly labeled "situation ethics," from the title of the well-known book by

Fletcher (1966), seems an appropriate way to conclude this section. Because Fletcher's admonitions are closely related to Christian teachings, additional discussion of this approach is included in Chapter 7.

Situation ethics, according to Fletcher, takes its basic premise from the Scriptural "Golden Rule," and its derivations. Given by Jesus as "Part Two" of the supreme commandment, this is seen as the ultimate and overriding principle upon which ethical decision making and actions should rest. According to his follower, Matthew, when asked by critics to state the greatest commandment, Jesus responded as follows. "Love the Lord your God with all your heart and with all your soul and with all your mind. This is the first and greatest commandment. And the second is like it: 'Love your neighbor as yourself'" (*The Holy Bible, New International Version,* Matthew 37–39).

As further explained by Fletcher, "Christian situation ethics has only one norm or principle or law (call it what you will) that is binding and unexceptionable, always good and right regardless of the circumstances. That is 'love'— the . . . summary commandment to love God and the neighbor" (30). Fletcher illustrates this with an anecdote.

> A friend of mine arrived in St. Louis just as a presidential campaign was ending, and the cab driver, not being above the battle, volunteered his testimony. "I and my father and grandfather before me, and their fathers, have always been straight-ticket Republicans." "Ah," said my friend, who is himself a Republican, "I take it that means you will vote for Senator So-and-So." "No," said the driver, "'there are times when a man has to push his principles aside and do the right thing" (13).

We may agree with the cab driver. But how do we decide what is the "right thing" to do? Fletcher suggests four "presuppositions" to guide our deliberations.

1. American pragmatism requires that an action *must work.* It must satisfactorily accomplish a desired end.
2. An action must be *relativistic.* Its appropriateness is determined by how well it accomplishes the goal of exhibiting "other serving" (agapeic) love in context (according to the situation).
3. An action is guided by *positivism.* Belief in the premise of love is accepted by faith, rather than rationally, although it is supported by reason. One cannot "prove," by seeking support from Natural Law, that love is the best basis for action any more than the hedonist can "prove" that pleasure is the highest good. However, natural law may be used to support one who "posits" that faith requires an acceptance of a divine law that establishes love as the basis for all action.
4. Personalism "puts people at the center of concern, not things." Things, including laws and rules, are to be used to serve people. People are not to be used to serve things (40–52).

Following these presuppositions, situation ethics "does not ask *what* is good but *how* to do good for *whom;* not what *is* love but how to *do* the most loving thing possible in the situation. It focuses upon *pragma* (doing), not upon *dogma* (some tenet). . . principles [are kept] sternly in their place" (52–53).

Arguments for and against Axiology and Value Theory

Arguments *for* value theory say that it gives us some options that neither objectivism nor relativism offer. The virtuous person develops skill in selecting from principles and/or consequences the guidance needed to make the best decision about action to take when confronted with an ethical decision. "Metavalues" are followed when they are obviously required. In other cases, one must choose from the "right" and the "good" (labeled by Hodgkinson as Type II and Type III values), with "care-based thinking" (as suggested by Kidder and others) as a variation of Type III values (the "good").

Value theory allows one to escape having to apply one particular theory to all situations. Philosophers who have tried to be consistent in following either the objectivist or relativist theories have had to develop various complicated and questionable variations of their preferred theory to deal with certain situations. Value theory provides the opportunity to use the approach that best fits the situation, with the ultimate goal of human "happiness" as the guide. It encourages and facilitates change and reform when current practices and habits have become obsolete and ineffective.

Objectivist and relativist ethics focuses on acts and choices to answer the question "What shall I do?" Virtue ethics focuses on the qualities, traits, and habits of the person carrying out the action or making the choice, leading them to answer the question "Who shall I be?" Where virtue ethics predominates, ethical awareness is a constant, even in the absence of an ethical dilemma (Jordan and Meara 1990, 4).

Arguments *against* value theory stress the difficulty of a person's having the experience and wisdom to make the best decision and take the best action without more specific rules and/or guidelines. These critics maintain that one would have to become a "philosopher-king," as in Plato's model, to satisfactorily use this theory in the real world. In their view, most educational leaders have neither the time nor the experience to operate in this fashion. They need more specific rules and guidelines to help with the urgent and often split-second decisions required in the real world of educational administration. These critics argue that value theory leaves too much room for individual preference and bias, even more so than relativism.

Another major argument against value theory relates to the fact that there is much variation among different people and at different times as to what is considered virtuous. As pointed out by MacIntyre (1984), earlier and later

Greeks, the New Testament, medieval and modern Western writers, to say nothing of cultures such as modern Japanese or Native American, include different items in their lists of virtues, and they give different degrees of value to the items which may be listed. As examples, Homer placed the virtues of the warrior at the top of the list, while Aristotle emphasized those of the Athenian gentleman. The New Testament praises virtues of which Aristotle makes no mention, such as faith, hope and love. One of the virtues exalted in the New Testament, humility, is even considered a vice by Aristotle. An often-praised early American, Benjamin Franklin, includes as virtues items which have not been mentioned above, namely cleanliness, silence, and an energetic drive to acquire material goods. It is also obvious that sometimes a virtue, such as courage, may be exercised to sustain injustice, and loyalty may condone unfair group practices (182–186).

Another point of objection relative to axiology and value theory is the obvious difficulty of ascribing motives to action. Does a person show courage in battle because he is courageous or because he is more afraid of his commanding officer than of the enemy? Is a person friendly in social settings because of good character or because she knows this is the best way to "get ahead"? Is one temperate relative to alcohol because of conviction or religious custom?

Case Studies

The Recruiter

A school district decided it wants to offer its parents more "choices," so it is determined that a new magnet elementary school will be opened. This school is promoted as the spotlight of the district. A nationwide search for the principal of the new magnet school is conducted and a gentleman from out of state is selected. The principal is allowed to work on a paid contract for one full year prior to the opening of the school so that he can hire personnel and then work to develop the curriculum for the magnet school.

As the new principal begins his work he "browses" all the existing elementary schools in the district to look for some teachers. Of course, the principal wants only the "cream of the crop" and does indeed invite the best teachers to interview for positions at the magnet school.

During their interviews with the principal, the teachers are informed that they will be involved in the development of an ideal school. The resources for this school will be well beyond those available to other schools in the district and there will be numerous opportunities for staff development in areas they feel are necessary. Many of the teachers in the district were excited about the opportunity to teach at the magnet school, and the magnet school principal got exactly what he wanted, the best of the best. Not everyone was happy, however, because the other elementary principals were not pleased that their teachers were "stolen." Many of them became irritated and began to complain to the

superintendent. When the magnet school principal was questioned about his
method of hiring teachers, he responded that it was not his problem that the
teachers wanted to teach at his school. "People want to be around winners," he
said (Contributed by Yolanda Williams).

Questions to Consider

1. What are the ethical issues in this case?
2. Should the superintendent do anything to control a principal's recruiting
   of teachers from other schools in the district? If so, what?
3. Do the principals have a legitimate cause for complaint or should they
   simply do more to retain their teachers?
4. What motives behind actions such as those described in this case are important from an ethical viewpoint?
5. What problems in the district are likely to be caused by this principal's actions?
6. Should teachers be allowed to move to schools they prefer?

Business As Usual?

Backcountry High School is located in a small, rural town with a history of
strong community leadership by a relatively small group of families whose
members are also among the more financially prosperous citizens. What was
once a rather homogeneous school population of primarily white students has
changed in recent years due to the immigration of lower income workers, most
of whom are African American and Mexican American laborers in agriculture
and a recently established chicken processing plant. For many years, the white
students have enjoyed special treatment and privileges simply because their parents elect the school board, which hires administrators and teachers and keeps
a sharp eye on school operations.

Mrs. Waverly is the new principal at Backcountry High School. She was
brought in with the express charge to bring school test scores to a high level and
improve all aspects of the school's operations. She believes that all students
should be held to high standards.

One spring morning shortly before the end of the school year, Mrs.
Waverly discovered that a suspiciously large group of students was absent.
Investigation by the assistant principal revealed that most of the absentees were
seniors, and they were gathered at a nearby farm. The assistant principal and
truant officer went out to the farm, where they found that alcohol was available
and obviously in use, with some students in suggestive modes of dress. In accordance with the student handbook policies and procedures, the students were
assigned to the Alternative School for five days. The Alternative School houses
students from the entire county who have committed serious behavior infractions that in the past would have resulted in suspension from school for a

period of time. Alternative School assignment also carries with it the punishment of being ineligible for student activity involvement (including athletics) for the rest of the six-week term. Some key members of the boys' and girls' basketball teams are in the group, and both teams are involved in state play-offs.

Soon, Mrs. Waverly's telephone begins to ring. The first parent to call insists that her daughter was not at the party (traditionally known as "senior skip day"). In fact, she had an accident on the way to school and one of the other students (also at the party) helped her. And, said the parent, she has already talked to the superintendent and to her brother (who is a member of the school board).

The next caller states that she knew where her son was and that senior students (sometimes joined by lower level friends) have done this for years—it's a "tradition." A father calls to complain that a group of students in a different ethnic group skipped and were not punished, because they were at another location and weren't caught. However, no names were available. This father also states that this has been happening for years and this is the first time the students have been punished. Besides, he says, Buck only had one beer! (Contributed by Letha Hopkins).

Questions to Consider

1. Is it acceptable for students to skip school because "they've done it for years" and parents are aware of it?
2. Should Mrs. Waverly upset the town's accepted standards and culture relative to "having a beer"?
3. What should Mrs. Waverly say to the parent who obviously lied for her daughter?
4. What can a new principal do to become aware of community standards and practices that may impact school activities and standards?
5. If a new administrator learns of "traditional" student practices that she deems unacceptable, what should she do?
6. Is the principal's memory about "sowing some wild oats" likely to influence her decisions in this matter?
7. How might the principal's actions differ in this case depending on whether she followed principles of objectivity, relativity, or value theory?

Activities and Discussion Questions _____

1. When a school administrator's values conflict with those of many in the community, what position should be taken relative to controversial issues (such as under-age drinking)?
2. Describe a recent decision you had to make as an educator that involved choosing a golden mean between extremes. How did you arrive at that decision?
3. Discuss what you consider to be the strengths and weaknesses of using value theory as a guide to action for an educational administrator.

4. Are there some additions that you would make to Harwood's list of virtues and vices?
5. Defend or refute the notion that value theory encourages change and reform more effectively than do either objectivism or relativism.
6. Interview three educational leaders about their preferences relative to the theories of objectivity, relativity, or value.
7. Select an issue from current educational questions and show how Hodgkinson's Type I, Type II, and Type III values would apply to that issue.
8. Over a period of a week or so, keep a record of actions you witness in your school that might be placed on the "excess to deficit" continuum. Which actions would you consider excessive and which ones deficient? Where would you place the golden mean in each situation?
9. In the daily life of an educational leader, how might the normally recognized virtue of courage become a vice? How does this relate to the notion of the golden mean between cowardice and foolhardiness?
10. Using one of the cases described in this chapter or one from your own experience, show how a person might respond at each of Kohlberg's levels of moral development.

References

Adler, M. and Cain, S. (1962). *Ethics: The study of moral values.* Chicago: Encyclopedia Britannica.

Aristotle, Nicomachean ethics. In R. M. Hutchins, ed. (1952). *Great books of the western world*, vol. 9. Chicago: Encyclopedia Britannica.

Durant, W. (1953). *The story of philosophy.* New York: Simon and Schuster.

Fletcher, J. (1966). *Situation ethics.* Philadelphia: The Westminster Press.

Harwood, S. (1996). *Business as ethical and business as usual.* Sudbury, MA: Jones and Bartlett.

Hodgkinson, C. (1991). *Educational leadership: The moral art.* Albany, NY: State University of New York Press.

The Holy Bible, New International Version. International Bible Society, 1973.

Jordan, A. E., and Meara, N. M. (1990). Ethics and the professional practice of psychologists: The role of virtues and principles. *Professional psychology: Research and practice*, 21, 107–114.

Kidder, R. M. (1995). *How good people make tough choices.* New York: William Morrow and Company.

Kohlberg, L. (1984). The psychology of moral development. *Essays on moral development*, vol. 2. San Francisco: Harper & Row.

MacIntyre, A. (1984). *After virtue: A study in moral theory*, 2nd ed. Notre Dame, IN: University of Notre Dame Press.

Mackie, J. L. (1977). *Ethics: Inventing right and wrong.* New York: Pelican Books.

Noddings, N. (1995). Caring: A feminine approach to ethics and moral education. In C. Wekesser, ed., *Ethics* (38–46).

Thomson, G., & Missner, M. (2000). *On Aristotle.* Belmont, CA: Wadsworth.

Pojman, L. (2002). *Ethics: Discovering right and wrong*, 4th ed. Belmont CA: Wadsworth.

Woodward, K. L. (1995). Overview: Virtue and values. In C. Wekesser (Ed.), *Ethics* (207–210).

Wekesser, C. (1995). *Ethics.* San Diego, CA: Greenhaven Press.

Ethical Decision-Making Process

We have reviewed major concepts from philosophy and ethical theories, in-cluding related philosophical domains for assessment of actions (action guides). Now we must come to some logical conclusions about how this knowledge and understanding may be used in the real world of educational administration. How may it be helpful in making the decisions required day-to-day, especially those decisions that involve some type of dilemma? In these kinds of situations we usually don't have a choice we like, although neither may be "wrong." Or perhaps we are in the pleasant situation of choosing from two or more accept-able choices.

In Chapter 6 we will consider the difference between moral conflicts (temptations) and ethical dilemmas, with some attention to the types of dilem-mas which typically confront leaders in education. The need to give attention to organizational purpose, dealing with ambiguity and using professional con-duct codes, will lead into a brief review of the basic approaches discussed in Chapters 4 through 6. Chapter 7 will discuss implications from religion, and Chapter 8 will suggest some conclusions and recommendations about how best to make ethical decisions in difficult situations.

6

Making Ethical Decisions

At the school where Angela is principal, the practice is to grade students' work according to their capabilities if they are officially recognized as "special needs" children. This means that special needs students may receive high grades on their work, even though the work would not be considered exceptional for regular students. A group of parents of these special needs children has complained to Angela that their children are not included on the school honor roll, even though they receive high grades on their papers and tests. This raises the question—what should be considered "honorable"? (Contributed by Steve Jenkins)

This chapter will explore ways to use philosophy and ethics to help educational administrators make better decisions and find approaches that are workable, comfortable, and defensible. To do so will require that you choose one of the major ethical theories and its accompanying "guide to action" or develop one of your own which may be some combination of these approaches. Before attempting that task, however, you must be sure that you understand the difference between "right and wrong" situations and true dilemmas, deal with the implications of organizational purpose, and face the challenges of dealing with ambiguity in the complex world of life and work. In addition, you will consider how the use of codes of conduct may be helpful in this effort.

Distinguishing Right and Wrong from Ethical Dilemmas

In discussions and courses dealing with ethics, the emphasis is usually on situations that are not "black and white." However, there is a difference between actions that are obviously right or wrong and those that may be reasonably placed in a gray area. As suggested by Kidder (1995), these will be differentiated as either "moral temptations" or "moral dilemmas" (17).

Moral Temptations.   It is dangerous to lose sight of the fact that some things are clearly right and some are clearly wrong. Those which are clearly wrong we will call "moral temptations" to distinguish them from "moral dilemmas." They are relatively easy to recognize, if not always easy to avoid because of personal interests or areas of moral weakness (which we all have). Kidder suggests that they include the following.

Violation of law is a moral temptation. However, using the law as a moral guide is both helpful and dangerous. It is helpful in that most of our laws have been enacted to enforce commonly held principles of moral action. They simply serve to remind us of what is right and wrong. Other laws serve the society by establishing an orderly system of government and to ensure justice for members of that society. It is generally accepted that it is right to obey the laws and wrong to disobey them. But then come questions about unfair laws, laws that may have been passed by prejudiced legislators or to serve special or personal interests. These kinds of laws are sources of typical moral dilemmas, and we will discuss how to deal with them later.

The danger in using laws as moral guides is in the thought that if it's legal, if it seems to be consistent with a law, it's all right. There are many actions that may seem legal, but they would be judged unethical and/or immoral by generally accepted standards. It may be legal, but that doesn't necessarily make it right. We must have guides to moral action in addition to the law.

Neither are actions ethical just because they are not illegal. As the old saying goes, "you can't legislate morality," and it is impossible to have enough laws, let alone enforce them, to make us ethical. Most people are intelligent enough to figure out how to do something questionable and yet avoid breaking laws if they are willing to ignore basic ethical guidelines. In other words, an action may be unethical, even though there isn't a law against it.

Departure from truth is also a moral temptation. Telling the truth is a generally accepted ethical principle. Failure to do so is usually deplored. Most of us have little difficulty in accepting this standard, although we may have some difficulty in always following it. Indeed, there may be instances where truth telling is considered by some to be unethical, as indicated in the previous discussion of relativism.

To get around strict adherence to truth telling as an "unbreakable law" of desired behavior, we may come up with statements such as "you should tell the truth, but you don't have to tell *all* the truth." Or we may manage to say nothing untruthful while failing to express the truth that may obviously be called for. "You don't have to say anything to lie" is possibly true in situations in which failure to refute a lie indicates that we accept a statement as truthful. In addition, we may use language to tell a truth that covers an untruth. It may be true to say "I didn't see anything like that happen," when knowing it did, even though you didn't actually see it.

The examples discussed above indicate that sometimes we need more than laws or even standards such as truth telling to give guidance for ethical behavior. There are too many situations where ambiguity makes a simple answer to ethical questions difficult. This is certainly true if one favors the relativist approach, because the situation may include unknown or poorly understood factors or the consequences of various actions may be difficult to forecast. But it is also true for the objectivist when language is obscure or cultural differences make accurate communication and understanding of a situation difficult. For example, the question "did you sexually harass Mr. Jones?" depends on how the terms "sexual" and "harass" are defined. Or if you happen to be a witness to a questionable interchange between teacher and student, the question "did the student show disrespect for the teacher?" may require understanding of how respect or disrespect is shown by those of a particular culture.

There are, however, definite standards of conduct that obviously are right or wrong. There are some generally accepted "Thou shalt nots" and "Thou shalts." They may not be as numerous as once thought, but some actions would be judged unacceptable by almost all members of current society, and we will discuss these later in more detail. As Kidder states it, these we might consider *deviations from moral rectitude.* According to almost all members of our society, they are outside the norm of acceptable behavior (Kidder 1995, 38–45).

Moral Dilemmas.   Although dealing with questions of "right" and "wrong" is sometimes difficult, many times the most difficult choices center on "right versus right" situations where each of the options is firmly rooted in one of our basic core values. A dilemma is created when we face a situation in which our values clash (Kidder 1995, 113). The origin of the word indicates its meaning. The Greek source includes two words. The prefix *di-* means "two," and the word *lemma* means "a fundamental proposition, a basic assumption taken for granted." An ethical dilemma, then, refers to a right-versus-right situation where two core moral values come into conflict, as distinguished from right-versus-wrong issues (113–114).

The choices available may each have some negative consequences or they may each have positive consequences. Either way, the choice is not easy, although the "positive-positive" choice is not so difficult to handle. It's the "negative-negative" choices that are tough.

Dealing with Ambiguity

As discussed previously, the difficulties in making ethical decisions often revolve around the fact that many aspects of human interaction are ambiguous—the surrounding circumstances are not clear, they may be subject to interpretation or cultural perspective, or their meaning may be uncertain. To deal with these it is helpful to recognize the typical types of dilemmas we face, the pressures which may create dilemmas, and considerations of organizational purpose and context that should be included as you develop a plan to guide your actions in difficult situations.

Types of Dilemmas

Discussions by Cooper (1990), Fleishman and Payne (1980), and Kidder (1995) suggest several types of dilemmas that involve conflicting basic values, to which have been added some typical examples.

Truth versus loyalty—when honesty or integrity conflicts with commitment, responsibility, or promise keeping. If asked by the superintendent to respond to allegations by parents that a fellow principal is neglecting policies relative to treatment of special education students, do you reveal information which supports those allegations or "dodge the question" to protect your colleague? You assured a mother that you would not reveal her daughter's pregnancy, but in the interests of the girl's health the physical education teacher asks if you think the girl is pregnant.

Individual versus community—when a situation pits "us against them," self against others, or a smaller group against a larger group. How much of the limited school budget should be spent on meeting needs of individual "gifted and talented" students to the detriment of "regular" students? As a school principal and a good friend of the superintendent, to what extent do you use your friendship to get financial advantages for your school to the disadvantage of other schools?

Short-term versus long-term—when immediate needs or desires are contrary to those which will probably occur in the future. As a school administrator, to what extent should you neglect building maintenance to keep the tax levy down and taxpayers appeased? Should more computers be purchased from this year's budget because of pressure from politically powerful parents of students in computer classes to the probable neglect of library materials acquisition for future use by the whole school?

Justice versus mercy—including law versus love, equity versus compassion, and fairness versus affection. Should the school attendance officer overlook some student tardies and absences that occur because the student is working nights to help support a parent who is ill? Should the assistant principal assess less severe penalties for rules infractions by a student who is from a difficult home situation and is making progress in self-control? Should a principal place a child with emotional problems in the class of a teacher who is better able to help the student than normal placement procedures would have allowed? Is the statement justified that "being truthful is important, but telling all the truth in certain situations is unnecessary"? Within each of the types of dilemma discussed above, various aspects of a situation may impact a decision such as the following.

Responsibility—dilemmas of discretion and accountability. As a school principal or assistant principal, which is more important, your responsibility to follow school policies and keep order in the school by sending students with behavior problems to the alternative school, where they will probably learn more ways to misbehave or become discouraged, or your responsibility to do what is best for the individual student? How do you balance your responsibility to provide for individual differences of students with learning problems and your responsibility to maintain standards?

Role conflicts—when the multiple roles of an administrator suggest different actions. As an administrator, your job involves promoting the success of athletic teams and also maintaining scholarly standards. What if a star athlete is disqualified before a big game due to a poor grade from a teacher who dislikes athletes and tends to give them poor grades? Your role as a community leader would seem to require that you accept a request to assume a very time-consuming responsibility with an important community organization, but your role as a school leader will be compromised if you accept the community leadership role, because there will be less time for leadership and supervision of your school.

Conflicts of interest—when your personal and professional lives interact and are at odds with each other. Your personal and professional advancement will be served if you accept a new job offer after you have signed a contract for the coming year at your current school. Your daughter will benefit from involvement in a school activity, but she doesn't really meet the requirements. Do you exert influence or "bend the rules"? Your good friend's son is a teacher in your school, but the teacher is basically incompetent, with little hope of improvement.

Defining "best interests"—when different stakeholders or participants in a situation may have different interests. There may be differences of opinion between parents and school "experts" relative to what treatment or school activities are in the best interests of a student with special needs. To help them learn to consider the consequences of their actions (and enforce school rules), will expulsion from student activities be in the best interests of a student who has violated rules for involvement in these activities, even though the student will probably drop out of school if taken out of them? Would it be in the best interests of a faculty member (or students) to pressure him to change classwork assignments so that there is a better chance that students will be successful?

Dilemmas of policy making—when policy responsibilities are related to other considerations. Conflicts that pit a policy maker's view of the public interest and the common good against what law or procedure require. Is it ethical to provide "leaks" to the news media which will support what you believe to be the best policies for your students? Do you "look the other way" or actively neglect certain duties rather than support policies with which you disagree, such as those dealing with corporal punishment?

Personal morality—when personally held principles of moral duty clash with utilitarian or democratic standards. Should the publicly flaunted gay lifestyle of a teacher affect your evaluation of that teacher? How should you handle the debate between evolutionists and creationists about how to teach biology? What is the proper place of prayer (or the Ten Commandments) in school activities and programs? What should be taught in health classes about sexuality, contraceptives, and abortion?

Democracy and obligation—when executive judgment differs from the majority will of the people. Does majority mean a majority of the nation, or your school district, or your school community? If you don't think the policies established by the school board reflect the majority will of the people of your school district (about censorship of library books or textbooks, perhaps), should you support those policies without question or resist them in some fashion?

Pressures Which Create Dilemmas

Various pressures impact educational administrators, causing ethical dilemmas. Scott and Wong (1996) suggest several of these kinds of dilemmas, to which others have been added.

1. Personal values versus school district values.
2. Competitive pressures relative to student achievement at different schools or among different school districts.
3. Desire for approval of superiors and/or advancement.
4. Pressures to provide desirable opportunities for students/teachers.
5. Opportunities for personal, professional, or financial benefit.
6. Hierarchical pressures resulting from organizational factors.
7. Traditional versus modern theories of leadership.
8. Admonitions of religious leaders.
9. Legal requirements relative to equal opportunity or "equitable" opportunity (affirmative action).
10. Responsibilities to family and/or friends.
11. Employee rights and privacy.
12. Status of women and minorities.
13. Free speech traditions (or lack thereof).
14. The tradition of "innocent until proven guilty."
15. Job security versus "employment at will" tradition.
16. Loyalty to colleagues, superiors, or the organization.

Organizational Purpose and Context Considerations

As we have been reminded by Goodlad (1979), Miller (1990), and others, schools have different purposes and objectives than do most other organizations in our society. Sometimes we tend to overlook this fact due to pressures from various sources to meet the goals of special interest groups and different types of organizations. Effective and efficient decisions in any organization are those which lead toward achievement of organizational goals. If those goals stress profit making, as in the business world, decisions may be somewhat different than would be the case in education or religion or social work, even in their ethical aspects. What is considered fair treatment of workers in a factory may be different from fair treatment of teachers in a classroom. The reward system with its necessary balancing of working conditions, salary, status, and intrinsic rewards must be adjusted to the purposes of the organization and the reasons for working in the organization.

Educational leaders must balance the interests of students, parents, and teachers, whereas the plant manager is dealing almost entirely with workers in the plant. The "bottom line" in business is the profit-and-loss statement, usually rather short-term. In education, the "bottom line" is student learning, success in progressing through the educational system, and preparation for future opportunities and responsibilities. Business leaders are often critical of the short-term focus on their quarterly reports, but this short-term focus is also increasingly being seen in schools (term report card grades and annual test scores, for example, rather than drop-out rates, employment success, or college entrance).

Educators must not lose sight of their long-term purposes of preparing students for life in the adult world of work and family and society. To do so becomes an ethical matter as legitimate purposes of schools are neglected. Standards for justice, equity, freedom, and attention to human rights must be made to fit the purposes and context of schools. They involve student maturity levels, abilities and talents, background and personalities, as well as curriculum content and promotion standards. Academic purposes must not be allowed to overshadow or even supersede those having to do with physical and social development, physical and mental health, the world of work, family, and "the good life."

Approaches to Making Ethical Decisions

At this point in your study, it should be rather obvious that in many instances there are no easy solutions to ethical problems. Our lives as educational leaders would be much easier if this were not so, but we can't deny the complexity of our responsibilities and opportunities. Therefore, we must arrive at some effective plan to help with efforts to make the best decisions in difficult situations. Several approaches may be considered, and perhaps more than one of them used in a particular situation. We will first consider the use of generally accepted maxims and principles (including rules and professional codes). We will then consider some of the recent suggestions about how educational leaders may combine or adapt ideas from the major ethical theories as they face dilemmas and difficult decisions. At that point you will be left to reach your own conclusions about the best way to proceed.

Maxims and Guidelines. A study of the various theories and approaches to ethical action might lead you to the conclusion that there are no generally accepted principles to guide moral action. However, throughout recorded history and within almost all cultures today there are some basic principles that are accepted. Kidder (1995) suggests that determining "what is right" generally falls to a code of ethics, such as the Ten Commandments, the Boy Scout Law, the West Point Honor Code, or the Rotary Four-Way Test. In seeking to validate these kinds of codes, he conducted interviews with world moral leaders, which resulted in the following list of core values:

> Love,
> Truth,
> Fairness,
> Freedom,
> Unity,
> Tolerance,
> Responsibility, and
> Respect for life (91–92).

Albert Schweitzer summed up the essence of moral behavior in the belief "that moral individuals have the same reverence for the life of others as they have for their own life" (Thomas and Davis 1998, 13), which seems to be another way to state the Golden Rule.

As mentioned earlier in this text, Aristotle identified four classical virtues, each achieved by identifying the golden mean:

> Prudence
> Justice
> Fortitude
> Temperance (Woodward 1995, 208)

Anderson (1997), speaking from the perspective of the business world, suggests six categories of individual ethical principles as forming the basis of most statements and providing the grounding for value choices, pointing out that the first five cut across cultural boundaries while the sixth is considered unique to western society.

1. General beneficence—don't murder, don't bring misery to others, follow the Golden Rule, self-sacrifice for a worthwhile end is good, improve the human condition.
2. Justice, honesty, and fairness.
3. Mercy or compassion—take care of others.
4. Frugality or economic efficiency—don't waste resources, protect the environment, follow a sense of stewardship.
5. Humility.
6. Individual dignity—people are unique, people control their own destinies, recognize the competence of the individual.

The addition of one more list of "ethical behaviors," as suggested by Wekesser (1995), is probably sufficient to give an overview of commonly held principles.

Honesty
Integrity
Fairness
Loyalty
Kindness
Courage
Generosity
Compassion
Altruism
Unselfishness (18)

Maxims and basic principles will be selected and applied differently, depending on a person's basic ethical position. These have been identified and described by Hodgkinson (1983) in a way that is helpful as one better understands "where they come from" and the basic approach to ethical decisions they wish to follow. He suggests the following "illustrations of the wide range of ethical positions to which a free agent could commit himself."

> *Guardianship.* The administrator sees himself as a self-effacing and dedicated agent and servant of the largest good, maybe even of the Good. . . .
> *Confucianism.* The leader cherishes an ethic of tradition, culture or order. He seeks to perpetuate through organizational means an ethic of civilized behavior and reverence for historical and social continuity. Extremes are anathema, haste dangerous, bad manners are to be deplored.
> *Social equity.* The leader subscribes to what has been called the "new public administration." He uses his office and organizational power to advance the interests of some particular group that he perceives as underprivileged. He is deliberately prejudicial on their behalf to the end of a supposed improvement in social equity or justice. Such an ethic would allow concealment and deceit in the service of its ideology.

Neo-stoicism. The leader adopts a strong ethic of duty and commitment to a set of classical ethical values in combination with an attitude of disinterest to outcomes and of non-attachment to rewards.

Hyper-professionalism. The leader sees his primary role, the primary element in his form of life, as consisting of a commitment to intensified professional values. He regards himself above all else as soldier or professor or scientist or artist. His vocation is his passion.

Human relations. The leader adopts as his pre-emptive ethic the psychological and material welfare of those with whom he has to deal within his organizational field . . . It is rooted in humanism and altruism in its basic conceptions. Sometimes it may take on egalitarian overtones; sometimes religious themes may predominate, as where an ideology of Christian brotherhood and love is espoused.

Religionism. All religions, sacred or secular, provide ethical systems to which the administrator can subscribe. Each or any of these may, of course, conflict with other discretionary bases for action and sources of value decision rules. As always, the critical factor is the stage and degree of commitment which can be ascribed to the value actor (220–222).

Codes of Ethics.   In addition to the codes mentioned above which are used to influence general behavior, specific groups and organizations often adopt professional codes which contain some or all of the items listed as commonly held principles of ethics. In addition, they are usually adapted to the particular group or organization so that the specific tasks or responsibilities of the members are more directly addressed.

Professional codes of ethics seem worthwhile, but they are problematic in several ways. In the first place, these codes are usually written in such general terms that application to specific situations still requires ethical judgment. The Statement of Ethics for School Administrators, as approved by the American Association of School Administrators (1981), illustrates this point. It is available from the internet site or state/national offices. Similar codes have been adopted by other groups of professional educators and most professional groups. Some attention to their statements may help you identify principles useful for personal guidance and other aspects needing attention and/or enforcement.

Another problem with professional codes of ethics is that they are seldom revised and the associations or groups which develop them have little if any authority or capacity to enforce their codes. Collegial ties among educators work against their being willing to "blow the whistle" on fellow educators. In addition, state and federal laws don't give them much enforcement authority and professional associations are either unwilling or too weak to be effective enforcers.

A third problem with professional codes is that fulfilling the obligations stated is often beyond the ability or control of the educators. The Code of Ethics of the National Education Association (1979) states as its first principle the following.

The educator strives to help each student realize his or her potential as a worthy and effective member of society. The educator therefore works to stimulate the spirit of inquiry, the acquisition of knowledge and under-standing, and the thoughtful formulation of worthy goals. In fulfillment of the obligation to the student, the educator shall not unreasonably re-strain the student from independent action in the pursuit of learning (285–286).

Social constraints, local priorities, or fiscal limitations may restrict the ability of the educator to follow the above admonition to "stimulate the spirit of inquiry, the acquisition of knowledge and understanding and the thoughtful formulation of worthy goals." Allowing students enough freedom to pursue ac-quisition of knowledge and/or vocational and professional goals may go beyond locally accepted norms. And school board decisions about allocation of funds to specific purposes (such as athletics) may limit acquisition and use of computers, availability of fine arts experiences, or professional training for teachers. The admonition to refrain from "restraining the student from independent action" may be disobeyed more because of local preferences and school policies related to zero tolerance than by individual administrative or teacher actions.

With their weaknesses and problems, professional codes of ethics do have their place, and they provide one type of influence on the behavior of educators. It must be recognized, however, that professional codes don't solve very many of the ethical dilemmas encountered by educational leaders. Other admonitions to be "professional" are also limited in their effectiveness by the same forces which impact professional codes.

Other Suggestions.   Modern writers attempting to develop a theory of moral ethics to follow in difficult decision-making situations take one of three basic approaches. Most of them propose some variation of traditional deontology, teleology, or virtue (including some who emphasize "caring"). Some have de-veloped a system that combines these in some fashion. Others rely on a system of steps or procedures to follow which tend to lean in the direction of deontol-ogy, teleology, or virtue, while including some aspects of all three. We will briefly review proposals related to each of these approaches.

Variations on the Traditional.   These approaches use different words, but one can see the similarities to deontology, teleology, or virtue. A prominent ex-ample by Hodgkinson (1991) suggests three "types of value":

Type I values are grounded in the metaphysical, in grounds of principle. "The principles take the form of ethical codes, injunctions or commandments. Their common feature is that they are unverifiable by the techniques of science and cannot be justified by merely logical argument. [These] . . . values invoke the will." An act of faith or commitment is necessary, and they are often codi-fied into religious or political systems.

Type II values are judged to be the "right," as distinct from the "good." The "right" is seen as "proper," or "moral." This judgment is made either on the basis of consequences or consensus. Rooted in reason and logic, concepts of the right are collective and social. "Type II values . . . correspond to the philosophical positions of humanism, utilitarianism, and pragmatism. They are buttressed by the social status quo, and the ethos, mores, laws, customs and traditions of a given culture. In general, reason and compromise are venerated, and the subscription to prudence and expediency makes such philosophical orientations particularly attractive to administrators."

Type III values, identified as the "good," and rooted in the emotional structure "are grounded in individual affect and constitute the individual's preference structure. They lend themselves to the reductions of logical positivism and behaviorism" (97–101).

In addition, Hodgkinson describes as "metavalues" those concepts ". . . of the desirable so vested and entrenched that it seems to be beyond dispute or contention" (104). The principal organizational metavalues are maintenance, growth, effectiveness, and efficiency. They are by definition "good." The question is always whether they are "right" (110).

Haynes (1998) suggests a "triadic taxonomy of ethics" which lends itself to "moral growth and maturity [by taking] . . . the form of an evolving spiral in which there is no prior value or end point." Using the terms "subjective" and "objective" differently than in deontology or teleology, the "taxonomy" consists of the following:

1. Consistency: a 'subjective' aspect in which one internalizes practice to see it as intentional. Here ethical action is deliberate, chosen, shaped and made justifiable by the personal coherence of internalized rules, meaning and values" (11). Kohlberg's levels and stages in moral development are used to form a hierarchy or developmental model to judge consistency.
2. Consequences: the 'objective' aspects of ethics which sees practice as externalized individual or social behavior, in terms of its causes and consequences" (11). Emphasis is on what can be observed, focusing on scientific or measurable aspects. It starts with goals, not rules.
3. Care: in which the carer attends to the cared-for in a special mode of non-selective attention or engrossment which extends outward across a broad web of relations" (12). Is there response to the needs of others as human beings? (11–14).

Haynes suggests the Borromean knot as an analogy—interlocking rings such that when one of the rings is cut, the entire interlocking system falls apart. In similar fashion, the three concepts of consistency, consequences, and caring are interconnected to develop a system of ethics (26). Ethical decisions must be based on carefully reasoned attention to three aspects of any situation:

(1) "What are the consequences, both short and long term, for me and others, and do the benefits of any possible action outweigh the harmful effects?" (2) "Are all the agents in this situation being consistent with their own past actions and beliefs? That is, are they acting according to an ethical principle/ethical principles that they would be willing to apply in any other similar situation?" (3) "Do they care about other people in this situation as persons with feelings like themselves?" (28–29).

Procedures or Steps.   Although there are obvious connections to basic theories, some authors have suggested sets of procedures or steps to follow in ethical decision making. For those who don't want to get too deep into philosophy or ethics theory, these kinds of suggestions may be helpful. A practicing administrator may find them useful either in selecting one that seems to make the most sense or "picking and choosing" from them to develop a procedure that seems most helpful.

To deal with the difficulties involved in using either deontology or teleology as a basis for ethical decision making, Green (1994), proposes what he calls Neutral, Omnipartial Rule-Making (NORM). He attempts to develop a logical approach to moral reasoning (from utilitarianism) while producing "results more congruent with our moral common sense than does utilitarianism." While trying to "capture the advantages" of deontology and teleology, Green proposes to do more than just combine them by developing a "distinct method with its own clear guide to conduct" (86).

Drawing on the thinking of both Immanuel Kant and John Rawls, Green tips the scales in the direction of Kant by establishing the requirement "that conduct must be publicly known and acceptable to all persons in society [as] the most basic consideration in the moral reasoning process—more basic, for example, than whether or not conduct promotes happiness" (87). However, NORM attempts to "provide grounds for ordinarily respecting the common-sense moral rules, [while also making] reasoned judgment possible when the rules conflict." It follows only one basic rule which is applied "contextuually in new circumstances" (96).

The basic rule to be followed is stated as follows. "NORM defines an action as right if it might reasonably be thought of as being accepted by all members of society as a moral rule, that is, as an abiding form of conduct known by everyone and open to everyone in similar circumstances" (87–88). Eight steps are to be followed in making the best decision according to this rule.

1. Accurately state the conduct to be evaluated as a moral rule (a form of conduct open to all persons in similar circumstances).
2. Identify all those who are directly and immediately affected by acting on this rule in this instance.
3. Reason omnipartially:
   a. Put yourself into the shoes of each of these persons.
   b. *Using as your guide their interests and all the facts you can obtain,* determine

      how each person would be benefited or harmed by this conduct both now and in the foreseeable future.

4. Identify all those who would be affected, directly or indirectly, if this moral rule prevailed in society.
5. Reason omnipartially about this rule:
   a. Put yourself into the position of each person affected by this rule.
   b. *Using as your guide their interests and all the facts you can obtain*, determine how each person would be benefited or harmed by this moral rule both now and in the foreseeable future.
6. Weigh *both* the immediate effects of this conduct *and* its impact as a moral rule, taking into consideration such matters as the quantity, duration, and likelihood of the harms and benefits involved.
7. Reasoning omnipartially, representing any and all the persons possibly affected, ask yourself whether on balance you would be prepared to see this moral rule come into being. If you would not, you should regard this conduct as *morally wrong*. If you would, you may regard this conduct as *morally right*.
8. If you have judged this conduct wrong but there are still good reasons for wanting to permit it, consider imaginatively whether there are various alternatives to simply performing or not performing the action, and carry out a similar analysis for each alternative (97).

As mentioned in an earlier chapter of this book, Kidder (1995) summarizes the basic moral theories under the headings of ends-based thinking, rule-based thinking, and care-based thinking. Ends-based thinking says, do what's best for the greatest number of people. Rule-based thinking says, follow your highest sense of principle. Care-based thinking says, "do what you want others to do to you" (154–158).

Each of these has various problems in application. With ends-based thinking, a major problem has to do with the ability to foresee consequences of actions. Extreme cases also pose problems for this approach. For instance, is it all right to kill a small number of babies through medical experimentation to benefit thousands of other babies? Or is it all right to condone the killing of a few innocent passengers to save an airliner full of people from a hijacking? Is it all right to neglect the needs of a few young people with extreme handicaps in order to have the money to better serve many with lesser handicaps?

Criticisms of rule-based thinking point to cases in which it commits us to absurd rigidities of following a rule because to allow one person to break it would require us to let everyone do it. It also overlooks unique circumstances that may result in breaking one rule to follow another (to lie to save the life of Anne Frank, for example).

Care-based thinking also has its problems. It fails to endorse particular moral principles, virtues, or ideals. It is too simplistic to be a supreme moral principle. For instance, it fails to give guidance in situations where both parties happen to like immoral things.

After considering the problems and criticisms related to traditional moral theories, Kidder comes to the conclusion that "there can be no formula for resolving dilemmas, no mechanical contraption of the intellect that churns out the answer. Yet, in the act of coming to terms with the tough choices, we find answers that not only clarify the issues and satisfy our need for meaning but strike us as satisfactory resolutions. [Ethics is found] to be less a goal than a pathway, less a destination than a trip, less an inoculation than a process" (176).

As a result of reaching the conclusion stated above, Kidder proposes nine steps to underlie ethical decision making.

1. Recognize that there is a moral issue. That the matter is not simply one of convention, manners, or involving other values, such as economic, political, technological, aesthetic.
2. Determine the actor. If there is a moral issue, whose is it? Is it mine, or someone else's?
3. Gather the relevant facts.
4. Test for right-versus-wrong issues.
5. Test for right-versus-right paradigms. This serves to bring sharply into focus the fact that it is indeed a genuine dilemma, in that it pits two deeply held core values against each other.
6. Apply the resolution principles. Locate the line of reasoning that seems most relevant and persuasive to the issue at hand.
7. Investigate the "trilemma" options. Is there a third way through this dilemma? Perhaps a compromise.
8. Make the decision.
9. Revisit and reflect on the decision (183–186).

Another set of procedures to follow in our attempts to be ethical is suggested by Hodgkinson (1991). Perhaps this procedure should be followed at the beginning of our deliberations relative to how to make tough decisions. But then perhaps it is a good way to end this chapter, because it is beginning to look like ethical decision making is a circular or spiral process.

1. What *are* the values in conflict in the given case? Can they be named?
2. What *fields* of value are most affected or most salient?
3. *Who* are the value actors?
4. How is the conflict distributed interpersonally and intrapersonally?
5. Is the conflict interhierarchical or intrahierarchical on the value paradigm?
6. Are ends seeking to dictate means? Or are means subverting ends?
7. Could the conflict be apparently resolved by removing a value actor or group of actors?
8. What are the *metavalues*?
9. Is there a principle that must be invoked or can that be avoided?

10. Can the conflict be resolved at a lower level of the paradigm?
11. Can the tension of nonresolution be avoided? (That is, must the conflict be resolved now?)
12. What rational and pragmatic consequences follow from possible and probable scenarios?
13. What bodies of value consensus and political relevance are involved, both within and without the organization?
14. To what extent does one have control over the formative and informative media in the case (press, radio, television, lines of communication, informal organization, etc.)?
15. How does one analyze the state of effect, and affect *control*, amongst the parties to the case?
16. What is the analysis of commitment? (Using the paradigm).
17. What is the interest of the commons, the collectivity? How can higher level interest be invoked? And how high need one go?
18. What, in the end, is *my true will* in the case before me? (136–137).

Case Studies

A Conflict of Interest

Sandra is a tenth grade math teacher and a single parent to three small children. She teaches in a high school in a large urban district that is teetering on the brink of being declared "low achieving" by the state because of their state-required standardized test scores. The school district has threatened to either dismiss or transfer all teachers and administrators at the school and start over if the school is declared "low achieving."

By early February, all of the teachers are feeling anxious about the upcoming test and the possibility of poor test results. After giving several released sample tests as practice to the students, the results show that a few of the students may not pass the test. Some of Sandra's fellow teachers are quietly talking among themselves that they are going to start looking for a job in one of the surrounding suburbs. Sandra is worried because she can't afford to move to another section of the city, she doesn't want to disrupt her children, and she won't be able to drive to a distant school in the district without neglecting her children.

On the day of the state test, Sandra notices that three of the math teachers who are acting as monitors are intently looking over the students' answer documents and test booklets that are on the table. Later, she sees these teachers erasing and writing frantically. As she walks closer, she realizes that they are changing the students' answers on the state answer documents. When the three teachers see her, one of them mumbles, "We can't afford to have these kids fail. Our jobs are at stake." Sandra hurriedly leaves the room, yet hears one of them say, "You know you need your job, too!" (Contributed by Pam Twymon).

Questions to Consider

1. Although Sandra is not participating in changing student answers, should she report this incident? What ethical principles guide your answer to this question?
2. If you were Sandra, would it make a difference in your actions in this case if you believed that the state test was unfair and potentially damaging to students?
3. Should Sandra at least try to stop her colleagues in their changing of student answers?
4. Are there other actions that Sandra should consider?
5. If students who fail the test are not promoted to the next grade level, should this influence Sandra's actions?
6. What might the principal or other appropriate authority do to help avoid this "temptation" of teachers to change student answers?

Policy Versus Students

Robert is the principal of an inner-city high school that has been recognized for its excellent development of curriculum and teaching procedures to student needs, resulting in exemplary student achievement. The previous superintendent and board of trustees allowed Robert and his staff the freedom to design the curriculum and develop classroom procedures appropriate to their students, with the understanding that positive results were expected.

Over a period of years, much time and effort went into writing custom-made curriculum guides. Course plans were developed according to the best judgment of the staff and adapted as needed to meet student needs. But then things changed.

With changes in board membership and central office staff, the accepted position of district versus school authority was significantly altered, with standardization and articulation as the justification. Policies and district rules were gradually put in place that required official approval of all curriculum guides by central office staff and the board. This critically impacted the ability of Robert and his staff to adapt the curriculum and classroom procedures to current student needs.

These new requirements posed a significant ethical dilemma for Robert and his staff. Should they follow the cumbersome rules about curriculum approval or "bend the rules" by getting official approval for a set of curriculum guides and then revising them to fit local needs without getting additional official approval?

Questions to Consider

1. Are Robert and his staff being ethical in their decision to effectively ignore district policies relative to approval of all curriculum guides?

2. Is it more important to go by the rules or meet student needs?
3. Are there other options that should be considered as Robert and his staff seek to find a way out of this dilemma?
4. Are the board and superintendent violating ethical principles in establishing policies of this nature? What might legitimately lead them to establish such policies?
5. Identify the role conflicts Robert is facing in this situation.
6. Are there "individual versus community" issues here?

Activities and Discussion Questions _____

1. Describe at least one situation in which you were subjected to a "moral temptation" on the job.

2. In making decisions in situations that create a true dilemma, do you prefer rule-based thinking, ends-based thinking, care-based thinking, or some combination of these? Why? Give one or more examples to illustrate your preference.

3. Choose one of the cases described above and show how you would apply either Green's "NORM" system for ethical decision making, Kidder's nine steps, or Hodgkinson's procedure to that case.

4. Describe at least one situation educational administrators often face that puts them in the position of choosing between roles that others expect and a role or roles they would prefer.

5. Give an example of an action that is not illegal but that might be considered unethical. Then give an example in which breaking the law might be considered "ethically correct."

6. Choose four types of dilemmas described in this chapter, and give an example of each from your experience.

7. Suggest how the differing purposes of private religious, private secular, and public schools might change what would be considered ethical practice by administrators or teachers.

8. Is it appropriate to say that schools "should be run like a business"? How would you defend your response to this question?

9. Suggest examples in school settings of the following practices which "depart from the truth."
   Telling the truth but not all of the truth.
   Lying by not saying anything.
   Telling a truth which covers an untruth.

   Are there situations in which one or more of these examples might be ethically acceptable?

10. Describe a situation in which pressure from sources outside the school have caused an ethical dilemma for you.

11. Develop and describe a framework or plan that you will use to make decisions when confronted with difficult ethical dilemmas. On which ethical theory or theories is this plan based?

12. Drawing from the different proposals suggested in this chapter about procedures or steps to follow in making difficult decisions, develop a procedure that you consider most useful to you, using it to reach a conclusion relative to one of the cases described in this chapter or another situation with which you are familiar.

References

Anderson, C. (1997). *Values-based management.* The Academy of Management Executives.

Cooper, T. L. (1990). *The responsible administrator: An approach to ethics for the administrative role, 3rd ed.* San Francisco: Jossey-Bass.

Fleishman, J. L. and Payne, B. L. (1980). *Ethical dilemmas and the education of policymakers.* Hastings-on-Hudson, NY: The Hastings Center.

Goodlad, J. I. (1979). *What schools are for.* Bloomington, IN: Phi Delta Kappa Educational Foundation.

Green, R. M. (1994). *The ethical manager: A new method for business ethics.* New York: Macmillan College Publishing.

Haynes, F. (1998). *The ethical school.* New York: Routledge.

Hodgkinson, C. (1983). *The philosophy of leadership.* New York: St. Martin's Press.

Hodgkinson, C. (1991). *Educational leadership: The moral art.* Albany: State University of New York Press.

Kidder, R. M. (1995). *How good people make tough choices.* New York: William Morrow and Company.

Miller, R. (1990). *What are schools for?* Brandon, VT: Holistic Education Press.

Nash, R. J. (1996). *Real world ethics.* New York: Teachers College Press.

National Education Association. (1979). *N.E.A. Handbook.* Washington, DC.

Scott, B. R., and Wong, K. L. (1996). *Beyond integrity: A Judeo-Christian approach to business ethics.* Grand Rapids, MI: Zondervan.

Thomas, M. D. and Davis, E. E. (1998). *Legal and ethical bases for educational leadership.* Bloomington, IN: Phi Delta Kappa Educational Foundation.

Wekesser, C. (ed.). (1995). *Ethics.* San Diego, CA: Greenhaven Press.

Woodward, K. L. (1995). Overview: Virtue and values. In C. Wekesser ed., *Ethics* (207–210).

7

Religion and Ethics

The elementary school of which Sheila is principal has been given a set of Harry Potter novels as part of a large donation to the school library. The students are very excited to know that the books can be checked out and several teachers have plans to read the books in class to their students as part of the regular reading encouragement program being promoted in the community. However, Sheila has received several telephone calls from parents who are angry that stories about witchcraft are being allowed in the school. They want these books removed from the school library and teachers forbidden to read them to their students (Contributed by Nancy Phillips).

The study of ethics and morality is usually based on the use of reason to develop norms of conduct. Reason relies on knowledge from the various sources that may apply and on social custom and belief. However, reason alone is considered inadequate by those who rely on religious faith as the supreme source of guidance in this life and preparation for that which follows. Among the religious sources used by the faithful to guide conduct are the Commandments from Jewish scripture, the Beatitudes and concept of Love from the Christian faith, the sayings of Muhammad, and the Noble Eightfold Path of Buddhism. These and other religions provide both similar and different beliefs and admonitions.

The Importance and Implications
of Background Beliefs

For most people, as they answer questions about proper conduct and make decisions concerning action, the background beliefs that inform and guide human
behavior are probably more powerful than reason. Few have extensive training
in the use of reason, but all are subject to many sources of instruction, habit, and
social influence. A brief review of how these background beliefs have come to
us today may help show their importance to current ethics and morality.

Aquinas laid the groundwork for much of current western thought about
ethics and morality as a part of Christian belief. He showed how the thinking of
earlier philosophers, particularly the Greeks, fit into the Christian faith. Plato
viewed eternal blessedness as the reward of the righteous, and Aristotle saw
contemplation as the divine activity through which man may attain happiness.
Epictetus moved closer to Christian belief with the notion that perfect contentment results from a willing conformity with nature and Divine Providence,
based on an inner detachment from the body and the outside world. "Man is
self-sufficient in relation to other men, in Epictetus' view, but he is not alone;
human will and purpose are not the only will and purpose in the universe.
There is God and there is Providence. Man is the son and kinsman of God
through the faculty of reason. Epictetus advises us to think of our affinity with
God rather than with the animals (through our bodies), so that we will use ourselves rightly and nobly" (Adler and Cain 1962, 78).

As Aquinas set the stage for modern Christian thought, he included elements that are also seen in other religions. Aquinas proposed that the transcendental end of human activity is the God of the Bible, who was revealed to man
through the Jewish people as recorded in the Old Testament and in the life and
deeds of Jesus of Nazareth as recorded in the New Testament. Universal ethical
questions are answered in terms of a particular religious faith, Christianity—a
faith based not on the poetic myths or rational speculation of men, but on truths
believed to be handed down by God Himself through a special revelation.

Aquinas identifies "theological" virtues of faith, hope, and charity, fulfilled
through the "cardinal" virtues of prudence, justice, fortitude, and temperance.
Acquiring these virtues will produce the "last end" of human life, which he calls
"happiness." In defining this "happiness," Aquinas argues "that whatever happiness may be, it certainly cannot consist in such imperfect, finite, or merely instrumental things as material wealth, public honor and acclaim, political or
social power, bodily health, sensual pleasure, or even the goods of the soul, such
as the limited knowledge and wisdom that man can attain in this life." It comes
as we achieve a likeness to Christ, which will be fulfilled only when Jesus comes
again and we become like Him (Adler and Cain 1962, 97).

From the Greeks to the present, the "virtues" are seen as leading to the
good life as they describe ethical behavior. As discussed more fully in Chapter
5, the "virtues" are seen as dispositions to act in particular ways, not because
there are rules to be followed but because the individual has reached a level of

moral development which requires virtuous action—with or without rules. So what is the relationship of the virtues to divine law and divine commandments? Aquinas brought moral thinking to the point of recognizing that "only a life constituted in part by obedience to law could be such as to exhibit fully those virtues without which human beings cannot achieve their telos" (MacIntyre 1984, 278).

As an underlying belief structure is developed to guide ethical thought and action, some serious questions must be answered, unless one is willing to accept without question the moral belief structure of someone else or some group. Nash (1996) has suggested the following:

1. What does it mean to be moral? Immoral? Who says so?
2. Is there a spiritual as well as a physical, intellectual, and emotional realm of existence? To what realm do you attribute primary importance? Why? Can you be moral and not believe in a God?
3. Would you characterize your moral philosophy as being predominantly rationalist? intuitionist? emotivist? naturalist? sensualist? theist? secularist? communitarian? individualistic? egoist?
4. Is an objective morality possible? or desirable? If yes, what is the object of our morality, and how do you avoid the excesses of dogmatism and absolutism? Or is all morality subjective? If yes, how can you ever expect others to be moral, and how do you avoid the excesses of moral relativism and nihilism? (41–49).

Religion and Morality

Does morality depend on religion? One view answers this question in the affirmative, another in the negative. Pojman (2002) differentiates these viewpoints as follows.

Those who subscribe to the **divine command theory** propose three theses:

1. Morality (i.e., rightness and wrongness) originates with God.
2. *Moral rightness* simply means "willed by God," and *moral wrongness* means "being against the will of God."
3. Since morality essentially is based on divine will, not on independently existing reasons for action, no further reasons for action are necessary (196).

If one accepts the above, then it is implied that the following propositions are valid.

1. [An act] is wrong if and only if it is contrary to the command of God.
2. [An act] is right (required) if and only if it is commanded by God.

3. [An act] is morally permissible if and only if it is permitted by the command of God.
4. If there is no God, then nothing is ethically wrong, required, or permitted (196).

The opposing viewpoint (which Pojman calls the **autonomy thesis,** standing for the independence of ethics) asserts the following:

1. Morality does not originate with God (although the way God created us may affect the specific nature of morality).
2. Rightness and wrongness are not based simply on God's will.
3. Essentially, there are reasons for acting one way or the other, which may be known independently of God's will (197).

If one subscribes to the autonomy thesis, as did Kant, for instance, then objective moral principles exist regardless of whether God exists. They are simply principles that make life worthwhile, and rational beings can discover them through reason and experience, without God or revelation.

Is religious ethics essentially different from secular ethics? Does it really matter whether one holds to the divine command theory or the autonomy thesis? Are they compatible or incompatible? Some would maintain that religion actually does moral harm and detracts from true morality, and indeed much immorality has transpired in the name of religion. Others question whether secular systems fail to provide sufficient motivation to be deeply moral. Kant, following the autonomy thesis, maintained that no difference could exist between valid religious ethics and valid philosophical ethics, that "God and humanity must both obey the same rational principles, and reason is sufficient to guide us to these principles" (Pojman 2002, 200).

Even if the existence of God cannot be proved and if morality has no need of God (relying on the autonomy thesis and "natural law" for its definition), as argued by secularists such as Bertrand Russell, theists counter that religion may enrich morality in at least five ways, even if the divine command theory and the autonomy thesis result in the same ethical principles.

1. "If there is a God, good will win out over evil." God is on our side, and good will win out eventually. This provides confidence and encouragement to pursue the "right" and resist hopeless resignation or even a noble stoicism.
2. "If God exists, then cosmic justice reigns in the universe." The question "Why should I be moral," when I may be able to get by with (and perhaps enjoy or benefit from) immoral actions, is answered. All people will eventually get what they deserve, unless repentance is seen as a way to earn God's grace and forgiveness for immoral acts. God's perfect judgment will result in reward for good works and punishment for bad works (unless I repent and am forgiven by a merciful God).

3. "If theism is true, moral reasons always override non-moral reasons." Secular ethics is unable to accept both objectivity and the possibility of an ethical principle being overridden in some way. A theistic basis ensures the supremacy of morality. Objective non-moral reasons may be overridden by moral reasons and superior moral reasons may override lesser moral reasons. For example, a good non-moral reason such as leaving one's family in order to help the helpless in another country does not override the moral principle of "honoring one's father and mother."
4. "If theism is true, then there is a God who loves and cares for us—his love inspires us." Because of a desire to please God, a believer has an added reason to sacrifice for the good of others, a reason that even goes beyond a concern for rewards and punishments.
5. "If there is a God who created us in his image, all persons are of equal worth." Without a belief in God and his commands there is no basis for the claim that all people are of equal worth, or that human beings have worth at all. If theism is false, it becomes even more difficult to answer the question, "Why be moral even when it is not in my best interest?"
6. "If God exists we have a compelling solution to the posterity problem." Beyond some intuitive feeling, the secularist has difficulty arguing that we have any obligations to future generations. Religion provides two reasons. God commands us to continue the race. He also knows who will be born and loves them already. We, therefore, have an obligation to care for future human beings just as we do for those living now (Pojman 2002, 203–206).

If the tenets of theism are not true, then it can be argued that the opposite of the above will probably prevail and man will be doomed to a "death spiral" which will lead inevitably into a deeper and deeper morass of immorality and human misery. Theism doesn't deprive us of the power to make our own decisions about right and wrong, so it doesn't deprive us of anything that might be desired by a nonbeliever. Neither does it deprive us of the right (and obligation) to continually test our faith through reason. Much evil has been done in the name of religion, it is true, so a religion based largely on faith must not entirely supercede a morality based on reason instead of revelation.

Barriers to Faith-Based Ethics

Religion as a basis for ethical action encounters several barriers, and they are not hard to identify. Childs (1995) and Braaten (1972) have noted the following as significant.

1. The secular belief that objective reason can lead us to moral truth along a path of neutrality, thereby avoiding biases and prejudice.

2. A tendency to equate Christian ethical ideals with a few commonly held principles (which tend to be stated in "black-and-white" terms, thus short-circuiting more probing moral questions).
3. The long-standing belief among many Christians that the spiritual life and the world of work (particularly the business world) belong in separate spheres.
4. The perception that the church has often been hostile in its attitude toward the "world of work," particularly the business world, neglecting to adequately address their specific daily needs.
5. People often accept a stereotype of the church as out of touch with the "real world" and incapable of understanding that world.
6. Church members, and even workers in religious institutions, are hard to distinguish from those who do not practice religion.
7. Doctrines and symbols of religion have lost much of their influence.
8. Technology and economic progress have surpassed religion in their influence on the average person.
9. The loss of religion and faith-based concepts leads to a loss of moral authority.

Appreciation for the Value of Religion

In spite of the barriers to faith-based ethics that exist, religion as a source of universal truths seems to be growing. Many observers identify, in the words of MacIntyre (1984), "a postmodern or post-Enlightenment era in which confidence in our ability to achieve uniformity of thought and greater control of life through pure reason by dealing with hard facts is being replaced by a growing appreciation for the importance of religion, ethnicity, gender, cultural relativity, and socioeconomic location as the ineluctable forces shaping our perceptions of reality in our pluralistic world" (29). He further points out that attempts to build a moral and just world order on the foundations of reason leads to "emotivism . . . the premise that all moral judgments are essentially expressions of emotion, of attitudes or feelings, both positive and negative, about certain behaviors and values" (30–31). This leads to the notion that "if it feels good, do it," "and a society in which people operate as though emotivism were true and live without the benefit of a unifying vision of true humanity [results in] a pluralistic world of diverse moral convictions and diverse versions of the human good based on a diversity of cultural and religious traditions and differences in social and economic location" (31, 34).

Natural Law

If we understand it adequately, natural law should support and reinforce religious beliefs if they are valid. Combining natural law with religious belief will then provide the most complete and widely acceptable foundation for developing ethical standards. In a pluralistic society, appeals to religious revelation or authority will not be accepted by many, requiring some other basis for suggesting that there are universal values that transcend culture. Natural law provides this basis if it indeed is able to identify universal laws for morality similar to recognized laws of nature that govern the physical aspects of the universe. When our understanding of natural law conflicts with religious precepts, then the believer faces the difficult task of deciding which is correct. In addition, as pointed out by Rae and Wong (1996), natural law is not so hard to understand as it is hard to practice. We know what we want others to do to us even if we do not always want to do the same to them. We may cheat, but we do not want to be cheated, and we may be dishonest in dealing with others, but no one likes to be lied to.

Manifestation of Religious Belief

As it impacts one's ethics, religious belief occurs at three levels (Kanungo and Mendonca, 1996). At the **cognitive** level, there must be recognition, understanding and acceptance of eternal values (or virtues). At the **affective** level, there must be an emotional bonding with these values, resulting in trust and faith in them. But, if the cognitive and affective are to have any meaning for life, they must lead to manifest **behavior** that shows consistent evidence of the person's willingness and ability to follow the identified and accepted eternal values. Our dilemas often come when accepted values, rules, and procedures, accompanied by emotional commitment, conflict with behavior consistent with religious principles. Rules and laws may become more of a hindrance than a help.

The religions of the world all provide some guidance for human behavior. There are many similarities among the major religions, so if religious belief is seen as a way to develop good principles of human interaction, it would seem reasonable to explore some of the more prominent beliefs of the major religions and think about how they could be applied to decision making by education leaders. No attempt will be made to delve into the details of religious belief, and it must be recognized that each major religion includes variations or denominations. But perhaps a "big picture" may be glimpsed from the best religious thought now available that will provide some benefit in understanding ethical thought and its application

Judaism.   One of the oldest of living religions, the beginnings of Judaism are dim and distant. The little we know about its beginnings is recorded to have begun with a Chaldean named Abram, or Abraham. Abraham broke away from the dominant religion of the highly developed Chaldean civilization, which was a merger of Sumerian and Babylonian beliefs. He rejected their belief in many gods, each supreme in his own sphere, adopting the idea that there is only one God, who created and rules over all that exists.

Through a series of revelations, Jews believe that God established a covenant with Abraham to adopt his descendents as a chosen people if they will be faithful to Him and follow certain beliefs and rituals. Some four hundred years later, He set up through Abraham's descendent, Moses, the basic foundations of Judaism (Gaer 1963, 131–135).

According to Jewish belief, God gave Moses the Ten Commandments, which form the core of Jewish law and ethics, amplified and built on by later revelations and teachings. In abbreviated form, they are as follows.

1. You shall have no other gods before me.
2. You shall not make for yourself any idols to worship.
3. You shall not misuse the name of the Lord your God.
4. Remember the Sabbath day by keeping it holy.
5. Honor your father and your mother.
6. You shall not murder.
7. You shall not commit adultery.
8. You shall not steal.
9. You shall not give false testimony.
10. You shall not covet (*The Holy Bible, New International Version*, 1996).

Although the Orthodox view may differ considerably from that of less traditional and liberal Jews, ethical standards are similar in many respects. Differences develop more in the application of standards along a deontological–teleological continuum, a phenomenon that may be observed in conservative versus liberal variations of thought in virtually all religions.

As mentioned in Chapter 1, Orthodox Jewish belief emphasizes rules to be followed. Less, if any, importance is given to intentions, motives, or consequences. Behavior must embody religious values, as laid down by clear standards expressed in divine law, tradition, and authoritative interpretations and, with few exceptions, followed literally (Kashar 1989, 129–135).

By contrast, liberal Jewish ethical teaching is built on the Golden Rule, and applied within an ethical system that relies on rational interpretation of laws and rules to fit a changing society and various situations. Liberal Jewish ethics relies on reason to guide action that is consistent with principles requiring that human life be treated as an end in itself.

In addition, an individual must have freedom of choice relative to religious belief and its application so as to make "the attributes of God into norms for human behavior" (Shapiro 1989, 168). This leads to a world view that stands upon three pillars—unity, diversity, and creativity.

The concept of unity is embodied in a greater unity, which Judaism calls God, "where part and whole are seen to be mutually interdependent." This unity gives rise to a multitude of interdependent forms, "much like an ocean supporting a multitude of waves." These forms are expressed in a diversity that at the same time encourages meaningful interaction and a sense of underlying unity. Moral responsibility thus requires "an equilibrium between selfhood and otherhood."

Creativity is advocated as the continuing activity of God the creator working through man's creative urge to "keep alive [a] yearning for self-renewal and to press it into the service of human progress." This leads to acceptance of the notion that fixed concepts of right and wrong are subject to review and revision consistent with the foundational concepts of humanism, rationalism and voluntarism described above. Herein lies a basic difference between traditional or orthodox Judaism, which "holds that God, creation, and morality are fixed entities," and liberal Judaism, which, without rejecting the past, "sees all three of these open to evolutionary change" (Shapiro 1989, 159–161).

Islam. Islam recognizes in Abraham a common ancestor with the Jews. It is believed Abraham had a son by each of two wives, the older son, Ishmael, being the progenitor of Islam and the younger son, Isaac, the ancestor of the Jews. The children of Ishmael multiplied where he had settled in Arabia and began worshipping where a spring had miraculously sprung forth when Ishmael and his mother needed water and where Abraham had later built a cubic temple called Kaaba (the Cube). In the eastern corner of this temple he set the Black Stone, which Adam had carried from the Garden of Eden when he and Eve, his wife, were banished from it. Around the Kaaba grew up a large city called Mecca, which became the sacred city for the descendents of Ishmael as they gradually took possession of a large part of that area. The children of Ishmael worshipped many gods and sacredness was even attributed to certain rocks, trees, and hills.

Superstition, idolatry, and depravity grew rampant in the land until the prophet Mohammed was born about 570 A.D. in the city of Mecca. As a young adult, the story goes, Mohammed was sleeping in a cave in the desert to which his family retreated during the hot summer month of Ramadan when he heard the voice of the angel Gabriel commanding him to read. When he awoke, Mohammed heard the voice again, proclaiming him to be God's messenger. During the following months and years, Mohammed began to preach what God had told him in dreams and revelations. Assisted by a scribe, he recorded what had been revealed to him and after his death these records were gathered by faithful followers into a book called the *Koran*, which means "The Reading."

The Koran became a powerful instrument, holding Islam together. To the Moslem, the True Believer, every word in the Koran is the actual word of God as revealed to Mohammed by the Angel Gabriel. Addressing itself to the downtrodden, the hopeless and the poor, the ignorant and the outcast, the Koran is given credit for the spread of Islam around the world. Based on the equality of all before God, it has had great appeal, particularly in areas of poverty and where people are divided into castes. It was also attractive to many because Islam did away with intermediaries between God and man, allowing the lowest, most ignorant or most sinful to ask and receive forgiveness and help from God (Gaer 1963, 193–205).

According to Islamic belief, "ethics is inseparable from religion and built entirely upon it" (Al Faruqi 1989, 212). The teaching of Jesus that the moral character of an act is valued for its motivating intent rather than its effects or consequences is acknowledged by Islam, and its ethical insights are confirmed with enthusiasm. But Islam claims to go beyond the teaching of Jesus to require that action should be designed to use science and other modern advances to transform the world. Others should be "invited, educated, warned, and adequately moved to join in every deed" but this does not imply use of force, as removing the voluntary aspect of good actions causes it to lose its moral value" (Al Faruqi 1989, 222). Among the teachings of Islam with strong ethical overtones are the following:

1. Ethnocentrism, nationalism, isolationism, protectionism, and cultural relativism are not tolerated.
2. Any diversity or political structure are tolerated, so long as they ". . . contribute to the preservation of peace, . . . to the . . . nature and enjoyment of God's bounty, . . . to the ethical felicity of the citizens." (Al Faruqi 1989, 231).
3. Others are judged by how well "they enable or at least require the people to give of their material, intellectual, and spiritual wealth to the rest of humankind. How open are they to envelop humanity as their citizens?" (Al Faruqi 1989, 231).
4. Believers in Islam should also practice charity and help the needy, avoid drunkenness, tell the truth at all times and under all circumstances, avoid adultery (including that of the eye and the tongue), be kind even to animals, show kindness to parents, slay no one except for the requirements of justice, give full measure and a just balance, and in judgment observe justice (Gaer 1963, 205–207).

Mashuq ibn Ally (1996) further explains precepts of Islam, elaborating on the proposition that the purpose of Islamic law is justice. He explains that "justice is a comprehensive term, and may include all the virtues of good behaviour. But the religion of Islam asks for something warmer and more human; the doing of good deeds even when perhaps they are not strictly demanded by justice, such as returning good for ill." Islamic law signifies the way to God, as given by God. The human condition must change in relation to the law, not vice versa. "Human reason is required to understand and interpret divine guidance in new or changed situations and to apply it to actual situations in human life. Reason is also vital to help frame rules, regulations and bylaws for implementing basic principles and injunctions and to legislate in those vast areas where nothing has been laid down [in the law]." Understanding of the law and how it should be applied is achieved through "forming opinion, consultation, and consensus by those trained in the formation and understanding of law" (248).

In conclusion, it is stated that the Muslim, by becoming conscious of God, "becomes aware of the qualities which will bring about moral goodness— qualities such as love, mercy, compassion, humility, forgiveness, honesty, sincerity, integrity and justice" (226).

Christianity.   Christianity also traces its roots to Judaism, as noted above, and the writings accepted by the Jews (particularly the Ten Commandments) are also accepted by Christians as descriptive of God and His instructions to His followers. Christians, however, see in Jesus of Nazareth the embodiment of the "Messiah" or liberator still anticipated by the Jews. Jews see Jesus as nothing more than a great teacher and continue to look forward to the coming of the Messiah, who is expected to establish rule over the earth.

Christianity as a separate religion may thus be traced to the birth of Jesus in about 4 B.C. Little is known about his childhood or early adulthood, and he was active for only about three years before being executed by the Roman authorities for insurrection. During that short period of time, Jesus preached to the people in the small geographical area we now know roughly as Palestine and instructed a small group of followers (called disciples). The principles Jesus proposed broke from the rigid rules and required practices of Judaism as then practiced, emphasizing the love of God and how this love should be practiced on earth. At its basest level, this was verbalized in the Golden Rule—do to others as you would have them do to you (MacGregor 1989, 193).

As Christianity spread and developed throughout the western world, somewhat different beliefs and practices were developed by various groups or denominations, but "its deepest meaning and value come from the metaphysical background or belief system from which it springs" (Gaer 1963, 189). This belief system proposes that God the Creator, through His infinite wisdom and all-encompassing love, grants to us as a trust the blessings of earth and life on the earth. This then makes it difficult to argue in favor of suicide or abortion-on-demand, for instance, because our life is not considered our own to do with it as we will. It belongs to God the Creator and was given to us as a manifestation of His grace and love. His power is not physical or political but a power made unique "by the self-giving love that governs all things from the deep core of divinity itself" (Gaer 1963, 193).

The unique love of God is proposed, most notably by Fletcher (1966), as the ultimate guide to morality and ethical action. Maintaining that which he calls the "new morality" is not exactly new, because its roots lie in the classical tradition of Western Christian morals; it is nonetheless a radical departure from the conventional wisdom and prevailing opinion. Fletcher suggests that there are three ways to make moral decisions: (1) the legalistic; (2) the antinomian or opposite extreme; and (3) the situational. All three have had a part in the history of Western morals, with legalism being by far the most common and persistent.

Legalism has dominated all major western religions. Statutes reign supreme and codes have been developed to interpret and guide daily actions consistent with their tenets. Codes and supplementary collections of rules have piled up in efforts to accommodate law to compassion and the daily necessities and complications of life. Elaborate systems of exceptions and compromises—rules for breaking the rules—have resulted in hair-splitting and logic defying foolishness exemplified by the Pharisees of New Testament times and similar rigid theologians since then. Still today, often under the label of fundamentalism, similar efforts result in a loss of compassion, logic, and appeal to non-believers.

Antinomianism reacts so strongly to legalism that it becomes an approach to ethical action that accepts no principles, maxims, or rules. Some forms of Christianity have taken this approach by reasoning that since Christians are assured of heaven in spite of their sins, then one may sin to their heart's content. The apostles Peter and Paul both warned about this excess in their letters to new Christians.

Other forms of antinomianism include those generally known as gnostics and existentialists. Gnostics are so opposed to law that their moral decisions become random, erratic, and quite unpredictable. Making moral decisions is an *ad hoc* exercise in spontaneity and impromptu reliance on individual feeling and reason, with guidance coming from within the individual as they deal with each situation. Actually a form of gnosticism, existentialism also rejects all ethical norms, axioms, rules, or laws in an attempt to allow individuals the opportunity to achieve their maximum personal development.

Situationism, the approach advocated by Fletcher, maintains that the situationist enters a decision-making situation armed with the ethical maxims of his community and its heritage, but treating them as illuminators of the problem rather than unbending legalisms. Fletcher's situation ethics recognizes that one must be prepared in any situation to compromise ethical maxims or set them aside in the situation if love seems better served by doing so. Situation ethics goes part of the way with natural law, by accepting reason as the instrument of moral judgment, while rejecting the notion that the good is "given" in the nature of things, objectively. It goes part of the way with Scriptural law by accepting revelation as the source of the norm while rejecting all "revealed" norms or laws but the one command—to love God in the neighbor. Situation ethics aims at a contextual appropriateness—not so much the "good" or the "right" as the "fitting." The situational factors are so primary that one may even say, "circumstances alter rules and principles."

Fletcher (1966) suggests four "presuppositions" as basic to situation ethics. These are mentioned in Chapter 5, but are repeated here to give more context. They are pragmatism, relativism, positivism, and personalism. Pragmatism requires that a thought or action must work. This requirement seems reasonable, but to what end? What is the purpose, standard, ideal, or norm being sought?

Relativism guides tactics, as pragmatism guides strategy. Actions are judged according to whether they work in achieving something. So there must be a norm of some kind toward which action is aimed.

Positivism brings us back to considering whether natural law or divine law provides the best way to establish belief. Faith propositions are "posited" or affirmed without the necessity of reason to determine natural law. Faith propositions do not exclude reason, however. They use reason to figure out what obedience to divine law requires in the way of action.

Personalism requires allegiance to persons, not things. Rather than the legalist's approach of asking what the law or rule says, the personalist asks "who" questions—who is to be helped and how? One is to love people, not principles or laws or objects or any other thing (40-55).

Fletcher suggests six "propositions" to form the foundation for situation ethics. They are as follows.

1. "Only one 'thing' is intrinsically good; namely, love: nothing else at all" (56). "Nothing is worth anything in and of itself. It gains or acquires its value only because it happens to help persons (thus being good) or to hurt persons (thus being bad)" (59). "The situationist holds that whatever is the most loving thing in the situation is the right and good thing" (65).
2. "The ruling norm of Christian decision is love: nothing else." Precepts of law are replaced "with the living principle of *agape*—*agape* being *good will at work in partnership with reason*." Law is reduced from a statutory system of rules to the love canon alone (69).
3. "Love and justice are the same, for justice is love distributed, nothing else" (87). We typically separate love and justice, relating them as love *versus* justice, love *or* justice, or love *and* justice. This creates tensions that can be resolved best by saying "to be loving is to be just, to be just is to be loving," using reason to guide actions (93). "Justice is Christian love using its head, calculating its duties, obligations, opportunities, resources" (95).
4. "Love wills the neighbor's good whether we like him or not." Christian love is more than romance or even friendship. It "is a matter of attitude, not of feeling." This means that actions related to others are guided by a will that recognizes the "neighbor" as anybody and everybody (103). "The radical obligation of the Christian ethic is to love not only the stranger-neighbor and the acquaintance-neighbor but even the enemy-neighbor, just as we love the friend-neighbor" (107).
5. "Only the end justifies the means; nothing else." Contrary to the traditional doctrine that "the end does not justify the means," Christian love demands that "love justifies its means" (120). An action can be defended only in terms of its results; "it only becomes meaningful by virtue of an end beyond itself." However, "if our loyalty goes more fully to the end we seek than to the means we use, as it should, then the means must be appropriate and faithful to the end" (121). The means actually become part

of the ends, as the ingredients of a recipe become the pastry. Good judgment is thus required to justify the appropriateness of means to ends. Both means and ends are relative.

6. "Love's decisions are made situationally, not prescriptively" (134). We are admonished that one should not "rush to judgment," when faced with a difficult decision, but the typical tendency to follow blindly some rule typically results in just that. Gray areas are ignored, or at best given inadequate attention. The legalistic need for order and a system of unbending rules results in lip-service to standards which are then often violated in the name of practicality, the excuse that "business is business," or expediency. The old saying that "principles are always sound but not in every case" must be given some credibility and "fanatic virtue" replaced by the concept "that actions are only right because they are loving, [and] they are only right when or while or as long as they are loving. The righteousness of an act (i.e., its rightness) does not reside in the act *itself*, but holistically in its Gestalt, *in the loving configuration*, the aggregate, whole complex of all the factors in the situation, the total context" (141).

In summary, situation ethics proposes that every moral decision involves four factors—the ends ("what is the object sought? what result is aimed at?"), the means ("what method should [one] employ to bring about the end he seeks?"), the motives ("what is the drive or 'wanting' dynamic behind the act?"), and the consequences in the context of the problem ("what are the effects directly and indirectly brought about, the immediate consequences, and the remote?") (128).

"Christian ethics or moral theology is not a scheme of living according to a code but a continuous effort to relate love to a world of relativities through a casuistry obedient to love; its constant task is to work out the strategy and tactics of love, for Christ's sake. God does not need our service; we only serve God by serving our neighbors. And that is how we return his love" (158). "Situation ethics keeps principles sternly in their place, in the role of advisers without veto power. Only one 'general' proposition is prescribed, namely, the commandment to love God through the neighbor" (55).

Hinduism.   As the first (and probably oldest, except for aboriginal) of the non-western religions that we will very briefly explore, Hinduism makes contributions to ethics from both old and new sources. It is, therefore, necessary to look both at the religious literature and modern Hindu expressions of the faith to develop some understanding of ethical concepts and practices.

Hinduism is often referred to as "a fellowship of faiths" because it has been to a large extent a religion of place (the subcontinent of India), showing an extraordinary tolerance to other faiths that have been brought into the country. One is likely to consider themselves Hindu simply because they were born one or because they live in India. There is no particular point at which one becomes a Hindu unless they are converted from another faith or unless birth might be considered such a point. It is also difficult to establish a beginning point for the religion, as India has been the location for intense religious activity for thousands of years. Influences have been brought in from without and evolved from within as the religion has passed through several stages or periods

Hinduism claims no founder, and no fixed creed governs actions, although a number of beliefs are held by most, if not all, Hindus. Having no fixed dogma or central authority or scripture, as pointed out by Menski (1996), "Hinduism puts more emphasis on action than belief, its ethical foundations being marked by an almost limitless plurality." It is "as much a way of life as a religion and Hindu individuals have a great deal of freedom in which to find their own path" (2).

Although there is considerable latitude within which the Hindu may find an ethical base, it is expected to be consistent with an accepted foundation. This central belief, according to Gaer (1963), "is that there is one Universal Spirit, or Eternal Essence, without beginning or end, called *Brahman*; which means, the World-Soul. This World-Soul is the Three-in-One God called the *Trimutri*. He is called the Three-in-One God because they believe *Brahman* is: *Brahma*, the Creator; *Vishnu*, the Preserver; and *Shiva*, the Destroyer." These are different aspects of the same "divine Unity," but they are not separate one from the other. *Brahman* also includes many other attributes, which have been symbolized and called gods, although the word "god" to the Hindu denotes a part of the one deity, not separate deities as in other religions. It is also believed that the various attributes of Brahman are "continually creating and evolving and changing the world" (17).

Focusing on Hindu conceptions of ethics, one may find some understanding of the Hindu value structure by examining the word *dharma*, which comes from ancient Sanskrit. According to Crawford (1989), "it signifies that which upholds or embodies law, custom, and religion, and is very much analogous to the concept of 'Natural Law' in its dynamic character" (5). Menski explains that it may also be translated as "religion," "law," "duty," or "righteousness." The concept of *dharma* comes from the ancient Hindu literature, but it is also "linked together with many other concepts to form a consistent body of Hindu socio-religious theories." These provide "a theory of the obligations of an individual according to his or her caste [socio-economic place] and stage of life" (4).

If Hinduism places such value on determining proper action according to circumstances, in light of only general guidelines, how is it possible to decide what is appropriate, and how are standards or rules established? Who is the final authority in such matters?

Contrary to other major religions, the sacred literature of Hinduism has little direct influence on the daily decisions of individual Hindus. This allows flexibility and adjustability to different circumstances and situations. It also gives the individual freedom, but not total discretion. In addition to one's conscience, the models provided by good people and leaders of society should be examined. If this does not yield satisfactory solutions, then one might consult books on *dharma* through experts who supposedly live according to its precepts. Divine revelation might be turned to as a last resort.

Although Hinduism seems to be short on dogma or moral requirements and long on personal discretion, there are some principles that are considered basic to ethical behavior. Cardinal principles observed by most sects are identified by Crawford (1989) as follows:

1. Purity—usually encompassing certain rituals and ceremonies, but going beyond these to the general purification of heart and mind.
2. Self-control—seen "as a means for harmonizing all of one's calls and claims toward the development of a happy and healthy personality."
3. Detachment, which pertains to avoiding selfishness and personal preferences in decisions and actions.
4. Truth and nonviolence, which "are combined and are regarded as Hinduism's highest ideals" (12–14).

To conclude this review of Hindu principles for living and ethical behavior, some sayings from Hindu sacred books may be illuminating, as included in Gaer (1963).

> Find the reward of doing right, in right.
>
> Make your acts your piety.
>
> Scorn those who follow virtue for her gifts.
>
> Do your earthly duty free from desire, and you shall well perform your heavenly purpose.
>
> Purity, rectitude and no injury to any helpless thing—these mark the true religious act.
>
> Right action is wrought without attachment, passionlessly, for duty, not for love, nor hate, nor gain.
>
> [A good man's] virtues, born of his nature, are serenity, self-mastery, religion, purity, patience, uprightness, learning, and to know the truth of things which be (32–37).

Buddhism.   Buddhism began in India about 2500 years ago at a time when the people were becoming more and more disillusioned with Hinduism and the miserable life experienced by the masses. Into this growing disenchantment with Hinduism there was born in the year 563 B.C. a prince in northern India. Stories of his life, including his teachings, multiplied through the years, typically including the following.

The prince enjoyed his life of privilege, marrying and becoming a father and receiving the best education and religious instruction available. However, one fateful day, while returning from a hunt, he became aware of all the suffering, misery, and death surrounding him. Then, encountering a calm and serene monk in the midst of all the misery around him, the prince made the decision to leave his palace, wife, and newborn son to live as a beggar-monk so that he could meditate upon the human condition. He immediately shaved his head, put on the monk's rough garment, and went searching for enlightenment.

For seven years the former prince wandered around seeking wisdom but finding no satisfactory answers. One day, while meditating under a wild fig tree and concentrating on all that he had learned from his Hindu teachings, a new understanding began to come to him. For seven days he remained under the fig tree gathering his thoughts, then going to the city of Benares, where he gathered around him a group of monks and preached his first sermon.

The monks were so impressed with the prince-turned-monk's teaching that one asked if he were a god or a saint. When his answer was no, he was asked then what he was, the reply being, "I am awake." From that time on his disciples and other followers called him Buddha, which means The Awakened or The Enlightened.

The Buddha organized his teachings and went about preaching and teaching. Many of the disillusioned Hindus became his followers, so that by the time he died at the age of eighty, Buddhism had begun its spread into the land and eventually throughout the East. As it spread and developed, Buddhism impacted those who accepted it and also adapted to local conditions and changing times, so that in time many sects arose. However, the basic tenets of the Buddha's beliefs remained basically unchanged (Gaer 1963, 39–48).

Based on Four Noble Truths, Buddhism teaches that there is a supreme end in human life that all rational and intelligent persons ought to aim at achieving. The Four Noble Truths teach that suffering is caused by human desire, and that this desire can be overcome only by following the Noble Path. This is described by Premasiri (1989) as the elimination of lust and greed, the elimination of hatred, and the elimination of delusion. The highest good is achieved by understanding and following the Noble Path, described as the "Middle Way," a plan for threefold moral training, consisting of virtuous practice, mental composure, and wisdom. More specifically, the Noble Path is usually labeled the "Eightfold Path," and consists of the following ethical principles.

1. Right Belief or View—seeking a middle ground between strict determinism and the view that mankind is free to transform itself, truth is sought as a way to improve the lot of mankind, avoiding a materialistic worldview and supporting the moral and spiritual life.
2. Right Thought or Resolve—keeping thoughts free from lustful attachment or greed, free from malevolence or hatred, and free from violent intention, one seeks to be calm at all times and not to harm any living creature.
3. Right Speech—consisting of avoiding false or slanderous speech, cultivation of truthfulness and speech that unites people, abstention from frivolous or vain talk, and use of meaningful, purposeful, useful, and timely speech.

4. Right Behavior or Action—including avoiding killing or injury to life, action based on love and compassion, honesty and forbidding of theft or fraudulent behavior, and abstention from wrongful gratification of the senses, especially relative to sexual conduct.
5. Right Occupation or Livelihood—emphasizing adopting of a morally acceptable means of livelihood, avoiding materially rewarding but morally unacceptable occupations.
6. Right Effort—striving for that which is good and avoiding that which is evil.
7. Right Mindfulness or Contemplation—preventing evil thoughts and giving proper moral direction to all aspects of mental, verbal and bodily behavior, assisted by contemplation of the Noble Truths.
8. Right Concentration—developing a clear and composed mental condition that will lead to the path of perfect peace and the wisdom required to eliminate all evil dispositions and cultivate the perfection of moral character. (Gaer 1963, 48; Premasiri 1989, 41–43).

The Buddhist version of the Golden Rule states: "I ought not to do unto others what I do not like to be done unto myself." This is expanded as follows:

> Under no set of circumstances does Buddhist morality justify the use of violence as the means for achieving some benevolent end. . .
>
> Hatred, vengeance, and animosity can never cease as long as they are met with hatred, vengeance, and animosity. These age-old forces of evil can only be permanently disarmed by virtue of their opposites. Hatred should be conquered by nonhatred, unrighteousness by righteousness, miserliness by generosity, and falsity by truth. Fundamentally the Buddha only permits a single weapon to vanquish one's foes—compassion! (Premasiri 1989, 52, 62).

To conclude this section on Buddhism and ethical concepts generally proposed by its teachings, a list of ten "perfections" is summarized as: giving, renunciation, insight, courage, patience, truth, resolution, loving-kindness, and serenity (Gaer 1963, 49–50).

Confucianism.   Having its origins in China, Confucianism grew out of ancient beliefs and practices of the land that emphasized nature worship and ancestor worship. Those who follow this belief structure seek in the records of the past guidance for their lives. Propriety and courage are given prime attention, rather than piety or asceticism, as in western religions.

Over thousands of years, the Chinese people developed a rich culture that included folk songs, rites and ceremonies, mystical drawings, histories of ruling dynasties, and poetry. This accumulated folklore grew vast and complex, with little order and definition. It needed someone to select the best, explain as necessary, and bring ancient Chinese culture into a more meaningful system.

A child was born in 551 B.C. who was to fill this role and develop what eventually became a major religion. His name was Ch'iu K'ung, and although he was poor, with few advantages, his intelligence and interest in learning resulted in his becoming a teacher and governor of great renown. Eventually, discouraged about failed attempts to establish lasting good government on a broad scale, he renounced government service and devoted his life to gathering from the wisdom of the past and passing it on to his students. He worked to develop in his students "a love for poetry, a sense of courage, regard for justice, and veneration for tradition." Stressing the importance of good listening and observation, he emphasized the need "to question anything that was ambiguous, until the ambiguity had been dissolved. 'Study without thought is a snare,' he told them, 'as thought without study is a danger'" (Gaer 1963, 77–78).

As he developed recognition for his knowledge and skill as a teacher, K'ung began to be called K'ung-fu-tse (K'ung the Philosopher), from which we get the name Confucius. After his death at the age of seventy-two, his former students and disciples assembled his sayings that they could remember, and although they did not consider him a religious leader, his teachings eventually formed the basis for the great religion of Confucianism (Gaer 1963, 77–83).

Basic principles of Confucianism revolve around the concept of *jen*, which may be interpreted variously as perfect virtue, moral life, moral character, love, altruism, and kindness (Tse 1989, 92–93). Moral goodness and perfection as demonstrated in the Golden Rule are central to manifestations of *jen*. This was stated by Confucius when asked, "Is there one word that sums up the basis of all good conduct?" He replied, "Is not 'reciprocity' that word? What you yourself do not desire do not put before others." (Gaer 1963, 91). Another wording of this maxim is translated, "Do unto others as you would wish done to yourself" (Tse 1989, 94).

Developing the "*jen*-mind" is the ultimate goal in Confucianism. This "goodness" is regarded as the root of four other virtues—justice, religious and moral propriety, wisdom, and faithfulness. It is also seen as that which distinguishes human beings from other animals. Goodness is the natural thing for a human being, evil being unnatural. Confucius, due to his belief that human nature was basically good, did not view evil as something to overcome, requiring the grace of some supernatural being. "Self-discipline, the study of the lives of worthy ancestors, persistent moral steadfastness—by such self-saving methods they could rise above the debasing power of selfish desire and so demonstrate the quality of jen, an inward integrity as well as an outward righteousness" (Hunt, Crotty, and Crotty 1991, 166).

Jen is ideally "unfettered, unbiased, undistorted, and uninfluenced by selfish desires and natural inclinations. . . . the motive of an act carries the most weight when the act is subject to moral judgment; consequences of the act count less towards its morality or immorality" (Tse 1989, 101). This emphasis on motive requires that a moral act be governed by the unique circumstances of each situation. Right and wrong for all circumstances are not prescribed by rules or rigid standards of morality.

In traditional ethical terms, the concept of *jen* may be described as more a theory of act-deontology. Although strict rules do not guide action, neither is a person completely free to develop their own preference as to proper behavior. Rather, one is required to follow established moral precepts, but apply them logically (and usually according to tradition).

Three fundamental and general principles proposed by Confucian ethics are described by Chung M. Tse (1989) as follows.

1. It is man's duty to follow the dictates of the *jen*-mind and to help others to do the same, with the final end of realizing a world of Great Harmony—a world where every person is a morally perfect individual. This is Heaven actualized.
2. If a man is to live up to the name of being human, he must respect his own person and that of others. To be respectful is to be respectful of the essence of humanity. Knowingly or unknowingly he is not to denigrate the dignity of humanity . . . [He is] not to act and treat himself and others in a way that erases the essential distinction between man and beast.
3. The cosmic *jen*-mind is in a constant process of self-actualization, and this results in the coming into being of individuals underlaid by a moral purpose. Nothing should be done unto a person by oneself or others which might suppress, subvert, or destroy the Heavenly potential he has" (102).

The sayings of Confucius and his later followers are collected in the Analects (selected sayings). A few selections will illustrate how the general theories and advocated practices of Confucianism were drawn from these and other sayings attributed to the "Master."

To see what is right and not to do it, that is cowardice.

The superior man is not contentious.

The superior man thinks of his character; the inferior man thinks of his position.

The superior man seeks what is right, the inferior one what is profitable.

These are the four essential qualities of the superior man: he is humble, he is deferential to superiors, he is generously kind, and he is always just.

Better than the one who knows what is right is he who loves what is right.

Fix your mind on truth; hold firm to virtue; rely upon loving-kindness; and find your recreation in the Arts.

Do not set before others what you yourself do not like (Gaer 1963, 86–89).

African and Australian Religious Tradition.   Developed and practiced by the aboriginal inhabitants of those lands, this tradition also contains elements of what we call ethics. When thinking about connections between religion and

ethics, we tend to think in terms of religion in the more developed parts of the world, those with written records and sacred literature. These usually come from the sayings or writing of ancestors or individual religious leaders. However, although less may be widely known about them, aboriginal inhabitants and their modern descendents demonstrate connections between religion and ethics as strong or stronger than people with a more extensive historical record. Many of the ethical traditions from different groups of people contain common, or at least very similar, concepts and practices. This may be seen with a brief look at religious/ethical practices among aboriginal inhabitants of Africa and Australia.

Although there are literally hundreds of African tribes with somewhat different religious and ethical traditions, most of them have a great deal in common in this respect. As stated by Ansah (1989), "no matter how many African ethnic groups there are and how different they may be from one another, certain religious and ethical ideas, beliefs, attitudes, and practices know no boundaries, be they ethnic or national" (241).

Both early and advanced cultures have been revealed through historical record to have a religion and an ethical code. These are preserved and past on in rituals, customs, regulations, taboos, proverbs, myths, art, signs, and various kinds of symbols. Stories and legends often explain the world in its various aspects and lie down principles for living at the same time. All of this tends to be close to nature, as it probably evolved as part of skills and knowledge required to survive in the land.

The importance of community and interdependence is usually a strong part of religion and related ethical precepts. It is accepted that a web of beliefs and practices connects people to each other and to the land. "Individualism is not encouraged since an evil deed by an individual can heap disaster upon the whole community" (Abogunrin 1989, 272). Whatever promotes positive community relationships is good and to be promoted. Whatever harms them is bad and to be avoided. Bad behavior is usually considered disrespectful or a sin against gods and/or ancestors and also a disruption of the whole framework that holds the people together in harmony with each other and with their environment. This is illustrated by Hunt, Crotty, and Crotty (1991) with the statement that "individuals are expected to share food, to show respect for the elders, to marry within the kinship limits, to perform rituals at the proper place and time, to punish wrongdoers" (192). Lying, vanity, and deception are unacceptable, and great value is given to maintaining peace and avoiding violence.

The strong sense of community among aboriginal peoples no doubt developed to improve chances of survival in a hostile environment. A Supreme Deity often is viewed as the source of accepted beliefs and practices, so an act considered taboo "is connected with man's acts to his fellow man, and to other creatures that are also of concern to the Supreme Deity and to the divinities. An act of inhumanity is therefore also an offense against the divinities and the Deity" (Abogunrin 1989, 27).

Aboriginal peoples tend to honor the elderly in general and particularly a group of elders given responsibility for maintaining the traditions and practices of the group. Ethical practices and decisions, as well as other kinds of important decisions, are reached by group discourse among those charged with responsibility for maintaining the social system. Others in the community are expected to follow these decisions without question.

Conclusion

Religion, in its root meaning of *re ligio* implies to rebind (Greenleaf 1996, 12), and it should serve that purpose in any context. Morality may not depend on religion, but even if religious ethics are not essentially different from secular ethics, religion can provide other significant benefits, such as motivation and satisfaction. It is also true that the theist must make every effort to avoid mistakes made in the name of religion—those that have produced obviously immoral actions. "Religion can be a force for good or for evil, but dogmatic and intolerant religion deeply and rightly worries the secularist, who sees religion as a threat to society." Our best hope for a better world lies in our ability to work out a morality agreeable to both theists and nontheists. "An ethics of belief . . . can apply rational scrutiny to our religious beliefs, as well as to all our other beliefs, and work toward a better understanding of the status of our belief systems" (Pojman 2002, 207).

As stated above by Pojman, there seems to be general agreement today that developing and following an ethical system based on a belief structure, either theistic or secularist, is important to maintaining a world society as we know it and developing it to what we would like it to be. Whether one is responsible for providing leadership in an educational setting or other setting, professionally or personally, success in the effort will depend on group and individual ability to develop and practice ethical decision making and ethical living in general. We live in a world that is shrinking and in which the behaviors of one group may strongly affect the welfare of other groups or of the world in general. Therefore, diligent efforts should be made to understand better the commonalities among the religious beliefs found in the world, as well as related secularist beliefs, that may provide a valid foundation for attempts to develop a "global ethic" toward which we may all aspire. Hopefully, this brief review of the history and viewpoints of various religions of the world today will be helpful to thinking about how they may each contribute to such an ethic.

Similarities and Differences.   There seems to be a general belief in the world that all religions are essentially the same, that "they are paths leading to the same goal" (Hunt, Crotty, and Crotty 1991, 195). As these authors further conclude in their study concerning ethics of world religions, "there is a great deal of overlap in the religious moral behaviour prescribed by the various world religions" (195). It is, however, difficult to classify such moral behaviors because different religious groups add a variety of qualifications—to justify killing, for instance, or to decide just who "your neighbor" is. However, six general conclusions from their study were drawn, a brief review of which would seem to be helpful in our study of religion and ethics. They are as follows.

1. "A religious ethic may be based on a profound awareness of God as the creator and lord to whom people are accountable." This supports the type of ethic with which most people in the western world are familiar, and its language of law and obedience are motivation to follow these laws and precepts out of a love for God and a desire to follow his will.
2. "Morality may be the expression of an internal principle or cosmic truth." This conclusion may better describe Hinduism, Buddhism, Confucianism, aboriginal, and related religions that lean less on an identified God or gods and more on a "right way" of living, vested with authority of tradition and honor to ancestors.
3. "The main thrust of a religious ethic may be the maintenance, transformation and/or perfecting of society." Stressed more by some religions than others, this concept seems to be growing in acceptance around the world.
4. "The primary purpose of the moral path, on the other hand, may be the attainment of an individual experience." In addition to benefiting the world, "living a good life may be accompanied by promises or expectations of blessings for individual believers."
5. "Religions differ in their view of the resources upon which people can draw to achieve their goals." This relates to our understanding about the extent to which humans may be able to rely on their own intelligence and strength and to what extent they must depend on help from a supreme being.
6. "Religions vary in their adaptability to social change." This conclusion relates to questions about how earlier religious laws and rules (supposedly originating with God) may be revised or adjusted according to modern needs and demands. Just how "black and white" is today's world and to what extent should older rules and ways be changed? (195–202).

Global Ethics.   Brief reference was made earlier to a movement aimed at developing a "global ethic" to gain consensus among the world's religions about more universal ethical practices. This seems to be a notion that deserves some additional attention before this chapter reaches its conclusion.

Global ethics is "a consensus among the religions . . . concerning binding values, irrevocable standards, and fundamental moral attitudes." (King 1998, 119). This is meant to be no more than minimal, leaving religions free to "express their own full ethical visions, as has always been the case"(119).

The ethic is based upon "a fundamental demand: Every human being must be treated humanely." Human rights are expressly affirmed. The ethic also affirms beneficence ("possessed of reason and conscience, every human is obliged to behave in a genuinely human fashion, to do good and avoid evil!") as well as positive and negative forms of the Golden Rule (119).

These fundamental principles lead to "four irrevocable directives" that serve as the following broad outlines for human behavior (Kung and Kuschel 1993, 37–39).

1. "Commitment to a culture of non-violence and respect for life." This directive enjoins behavior that respects the human rights to "life safety, and the free development of personality," declaring that conflicts "should be resolved without violence within a framework of justice."
2. "Commitment to a culture of solidarity and a just economic order." Based upon ancient religious codes that state: "You shall not steal!" (or, in positive terms: "Deal honestly and fairly!") this directive states: "No one has the right to rob or dispossess in any way whatsoever any other person or the commonwealth. Further, no one has the right to use her or his possessions without concern for the needs of society and Earth."
3. "Commitment to a culture of tolerance and a life of truthfulness." Based upon ancient religious codes that declare: "You shall not lie!" (or, in positive terms: "Speak and act truthfully!") this directive applies to everyone, but it singles out as bearing especially great responsibility for truthfulness persons who work for the mass media; artists, writers, and scientists; the leaders of countries; politicians and political parties; and representatives of religion.
4. "Commitment to a culture of equal rights and partnership between men and women. [This] directive condemns all forms of sexual exploitation and sexual discrimination. . . ."

Whether a person accepts religious belief or not, it seems reasonable to state that the present and future promise of a hope that may be gained from belief in religious principles "is our bulwark against moral cynicism and discouragement as we struggle for whatever gains we can make in this world. All the penultimate, day-to-day moments of caring and service—of going beyond the moral minimum, beyond excellence to virtue, beyond affirmative action to true community, beyond mere survival to care for the earth, and beyond complacent certainty to the embrace of faith—bear witness to that radical, ultimate promise" (adapted from Childs 1995, 148).

Case Studies

More Than Meets the Eye

Mr. Roosevelt is a popular teacher and coach at Oakwood High School. He is known for his flamboyant coaching style, which has yielded him a very productive career not only at Oakwood, but also at several other schools in the region.

A veteran coach, he is only two years from retirement. A hobby that he is known for throughout the district is photography, his subject often being high school students.

Mr. Rider is the principal of Oakwood High, and has known Mr. Roosevelt for a number of years. Consequently, when Mr. Roosevelt decided he needed a change of environment and a less stressful coaching situation, he asked to be transferred to Mr. Rider's school. Mr. Rider gladly agreed, because Mr. Roosevelt was good with students and was a supporter of Mr. Rider.

One day while Mr. Rider was visiting Mr. Roosevelt's room, he noticed several photographs of Oakwood students on the bulletin board, in what Mr. Rider considered to be sexually suggestive poses. When he questioned Mr. Roosevelt about them, Mr. Roosevelt said that he saw nothing wrong with the pictures, and that he had been taking these kinds of pictures for years. Besides, the students took them all in fun and no one had ever questioned him before about these kinds of bulletin board pictures. Moreover, when he retired he was thinking about setting up his own photography studio.

Mr. Rider was uncertain about what he should do about this situation. There had already been some controversy in the community about prayer at football games and the school dress code, which was rather severe, and he didn't want to stir up any more trouble. After all, he was also only two years from retirement. (Contributed by Aubrey Todd).

Questions to Consider

1. What are the ethical questions involved in this case?
2. If the students in the pictures were all at least eighteen years of age, would this alter the situation?
3. What courses of action might Mr. Rider appropriately consider?
4. Should the general level of acceptability in the community relative to moral standards have anything to do with Mr. Rider's actions?
5. What action should Mr. Rider take? How could he justify this action to the superintendent and school board?

Truth or Student?

Josh is one of those students who are "marginal" relative to being qualified for special services. His test scores indicate that he probably has the ability to do regular schoolwork, but his home situation and past school experiences negatively impact his school achievement. As required by law, a committee has been set up to consider Josh's case and recommend any special services or consideration that he should receive in school. One of the concerns addressed by the committee is whether Josh should be held to the same standards as other students relative to participation in student activities—including athletics. Another is whether he should be given special help with developing his reading skills.

Josh happens to be a very good athlete, and football is about the only thing about school that provides some success for him. His parents seem to have little interest in whether Josh is successful in school; in fact, his father would like for him to drop out and help with his lawn service business.

The committee meets to decide whether Josh should receive special services and consideration because of his mental ability. After looking at test scores and considering various aspects of the case, the committee votes three to two not to provide special services or allow special considerations relative to student activities participation. A major impact on the committee's decision was the fact that the special reading teacher was already overloaded and there were other students with more serious problems. The majority of the committee also felt that Josh should devote more time to his academic studies rather than participate in athletics.

Alvin Newcomer is the first-year assistant principal at Josh's high school, and one of his responsibilities is to certify the eligibility of students to participate in interscholastic athletics. This is a "football town," and the team is entering the play-offs for the state championship. Josh is a key player, and his back-up was injured in the last game. To his dismay, Mr. Newcomer learns when preparing the eligibility list for the play-off game that the computer class teacher and the mathematics teacher have reported Josh as failing. This makes Josh ineligible for the "big game," unless he is allowed exemption from the regular academic requirements as a special student. One failing class is acceptable, but two failures makes him ineligible.

Mr. Newcomer talks to both of the teachers who reported Josh to be failing and learned that he was "on the borderline" in both classes. Both teachers reported that Josh was making a reasonable effort, but that his absences due to football games had probably caused the failures this term.

Questions to Consider

1. What are the options for action that Mr. Newcomer might consider?
2. What are the ethical issues most prominent in this case?
3. Should Mr. Newcomer pressure the teachers who reported the failing grades to reconsider?
4. Should Mr. Newcomer convene the committee to reconsider Josh's status as a special student and try to persuade them to change their decision?
5. Should Mr. Newcomer "lose" the report from the computer teacher?
6. Are there some options for school policy and procedures that might help avoid this kind of dilemma in the future?
7. Should Mr. Newcomer have put Josh in the special reading group even though the appropriate committee did not recommend it?

Activities and Discussion Questions _____

1. What common practices in school settings are manifestations of religious beliefs?

2. Interview one or more educational administrators and ask about when and why they have applied situation ethics.

3. Why do teachers and administrators sometimes compromise ethical maxims?

4. State the major arguments about whether morality can exist without religion.

5. Compare and contrast how a religion other than Christianity may contribute to ethical thought.

6. State and support your position relative to whether you subscribe to the divine command theory or the autonomy thesis.

7. Give examples of how barriers to faith-based ethics may exist in school settings.

8. There are strong traditions and laws in this country relative to the separation of church and state. Argue the merits and problems with this concept as currently practiced in our schools. Include examples of difficulties faced by educational administrators because of these traditions and laws.

9. Are there potential problems in using Christian principles to drive ethical decisions in educational settings? If so, suggest some examples.

10. Can religion conflict with morality? If so, suggest some examples in educational settings.

11. Describe one or more ethical dilemmas that may be encountered by educational administrators in dealing with religion and religious issues.

12. Are there times when religious ethics may conflict with secular ethics? If so, suggest some examples, particularly in educational settings.

13. What does it mean to be moral?

14. Discuss how one's ethics might exist at the cognitive, affective, and behavioral levels.

15. Identify those principles that seem to be common among all major world religions.

16. Describe what seem to be major differences among some world religions relative to ethical principles.

References _____

Adler, M. and Cain, S. (1962). *Ethics: The study of moral values.* Chicago: Encyclopedia Britannica.

Al Faruqi, I. R. (1989). Islamic ethics. In S. C. Crawford, ed. *World religions and global ethics* (212–237). New York: Paragon House.

Ally, M. (1996). Islam. In P. Morgan & C. Lawton, eds. *Ethical issues in six religious traditions* (220–263). Edinburgh: Edinburgh University Press.

Abogunrin, S. O. (1989). Ethics in Yoruba religious tradition. In S. C. Crawford, ed. *World religions and global ethics* (266–296). New York: Paragon House

Ansah, J. K. (1989). The ethics of African religious tradition. In S. C. Crawford ed. *World religion and global ethics* (241–265). New York: Paragon House

Braaten, C.E. (1972) *Christ and counter-Christ.* Philadelphia: Fortress Press.

Childs, J. M., Jr. (1995). *Ethics in business: Faith at work.* Minneapolis: Fortress Press.

Crawford, S. C., ed. (1989). *World religions and global ethics.* New York: Paragon House.

Fletcher, J. (1966). *Situation ethics.* Philadelphia: The Westminster Press.

Gaer, J. (1963). *What the great religions believe.* New York: Dodd, Mead & Co.

Greenleaf, R. K. (1996). *Seeker and servant: Reflections on religious leadership.* A. T. Fraker and L. C. Spears, eds. San Francisco: Jossey-Bass.

The Holy Bible, New International Version. (1996). Grand Rapids, MI: Zondervan Publishing House.

Hunt, A. D., Crotty, M. T., and Crotty, R. B. (1991). *Ethics of world religions* (revised). San Diego, CA: Greenhaven Press.

Kasher, A. (1989). Jewish ethics: Orthodox view. In S. C. Crawford, ed. *World religions and global ethics* (129–154). New York: Paragon House.

King, S. (1998). A global ethic in the light of comparative religious ethics. In S. B. Twiss & B. Grelle, eds. *Explorations in global ethics* (118–140). Boulder, Co: Westview Press.

Kung, H. and Kuschel, K., eds. (1993). A global ethic: The declaration of the parliament of the world's religions. In S. B. Twiss and B. Grelle, eds. *Explorations in global ethics* (118–121). Boulder, Co: Westview Press

MacGregor, G. (1989). Ethical consequences of the Christian way. In S. C. Crawford, ed. *World religions and global ethics* (188–211). New York: Paragon House.

MacIntyre, A. (1984). *After virtue: A study in moral theory, (2nd ed.)* Notre Dame, IN: University of Notre Dame Press.

Menski, W. (1996). Hinduism. In P. Morgan & C. Lawton, eds. *Ethical issues in six religious traditions* (1–54). Edinburgh: Edinburgh University Press.

Morgan, P. and Lawton, C., eds. (1996). *Ethical issues in six religious traditions.* Edinburgh: Edinburgh University Press.

Nash, R. J. (1996). *Real world ethics.* New York: Teachers College Press.

The New English Bible. (1970). New York: Oxford University Press.

Pojman, L. P. (2002). *Ethics: Discovering Right and Wrong, 4th ed.* Belmont, CA: Wadsworth.

Premasiri, P. E. (1989). Ethics in the Theravada Buddhist tradition. In S. C. Crawford, ed. *World religions and global ethics.* (37–64). New York: Paragon House.

Rae, S. B., and Wong, K. L. (1996). *Beyond integrity: A Judeo-Christian approach to business ethics.* Grand Rapids, MI: Zondervan.

Shapiro, R. M. (1989). Blessing and curse: Toward a liberal Jewish ethic. In S. C. Crawford, ed. *World religions and global ethics* (155–187). New York: Paragon House

Tse, C. M. (1989). Confucianism and contemporary ethical issues. In S. C. Crawford (ed.). *World religions and global ethics* (92–125). New York: Paragon House.

Twiss, S. B., and Grelle, B., eds. (1998). *Explorations in global ethics.* Boulder, CO: Westview Press.

8

So What?
Conclusions and Suggestions

Warren has been superintendent of a small rural school district in the midwest for five years, and things seem to be going well. However, a sticky situation has been presented to him by the principal of the elementary school. One of the teachers, a young, single lady, who is known to be a good teacher, has revealed that she is pregnant by a man she has been living with, and they have no plans to get married. She is opposed to abortion and plans to keep the baby. There has been talk in the community about this "live-in" situation for some time, but this development adds a complicating factor.

We now come to the point of more directly discussing how the theories, information, and thoughts about ethics and ethical leadership contained in Chapters 1 through 7 might best be used to improve leadership by school administrators, with the ultimate purpose of improving educational opportunities for those enrolled in our schools. Many ideas and historical developments have been described and illustrated throughout the book. Now it is time to "go out on a limb" and suggest what seem to be the best choices among alternative approaches to making ethical decisions, and how these choices should be applied. Some might say that this is not the purpose of a textbook, that the author's place is to simply supply information and leave readers to reach their own conclusions about the best choices to make among competing or contrasting ideas. This may be so, but the author has a habit of asking "so what?" What is the best use of scholarly thought as educational administrators go about their daily tasks? What difference will it make? Some personal biases will be obvious, but having asked the question, it seems appropriate to suggest some answers as ethical theory and scholarly thought are applied to daily practice. If nothing else, perhaps these suggestions will stimulate further thought and reflection by those who read this book.

To cope with the daily challenges of organizational administration, particularly in education, one must have a workable set of principles and convictions from which to operate. An extensive process of philosophical debate through which one must work before making a decision is not practical, but a basic understanding of ethical theory and how to apply it to everyday decision-making is necessary. As pointed out by Hodgkinson (1983), leadership has been more a subdivision of psychology than philosophy (198), but the best administrators for the future will be able to combine and synthesize approaches from both psychology and philosophy as they reconcile the "nomothetic" and the "idiographic" conflicts within an organization. They will be able to provide appropriate leadership as educational professionals resolve the continuous tension between organizational purposes and human concerns.

The School as an Ethical and Democratic Community

What are schools for? This basic, if somewhat ungrammatical, question is fundamental to all we do as educators and educational leaders. There are several angles from which this question must be answered. We will consider only the perspective that involves ethical questions and considerations, and the "bedrock" of this perspective is found in principles of democracy and a democratic society.

Identifying democracy as the basic concept to be followed by ethical educators is easy enough and not subject to very much controversy. Identifying the more specific ethical principles and practices that must be followed is not so easy. Although the term is generally applied to a type of government, it is also applied to a general attitude, a way of operating within a society or culture. As related to government, we generally understand democracy to mean a system in which the people exercise political power through a representative arrangement. A definition more related to our discussion here identifies democracy as "a state of society characterized by formal equality of rights and privileges; political or social equality" (*Random House Webster's College Dictionary* 1992, 360). Modern concepts include the operating presence of inalienable rights, and philosophers of democracy generally emphasize the spread of education as being essential to an effective democratic society.

An effective democracy also requires the active participation of its citizens in the processes of government, combined with effective delegation of power and responsibility. John Dewey, although known as a prominent educational philosopher and theoretician, is recognized as one who stressed the importance of participation in day-to-day political affairs at all levels of local, state, and national government. This has resulted in the concept of democracy being extended so that it may be understood to be both a political and an ethical term.

Ethical concepts of democracy propose that "the institutions of society are geared to manifest an equality of concern for all human beings to develop the fullest reach of their powers" (*The Encyclopedia Americana, International Edition* 1986, vol. 8, 686). In addition, modern concepts of democracy propose that human beings who are affected by decisions should have some say in influencing those decisions, with a question then becoming apparent as to whether this means only consultation or actual shared responsibility in making the decision.

During the last century, John Dewey has been the most influential philosopher and theoretician concerning the application of democratic principles to education. He discussed two criteria for a good society, both of which "point to democracy," maintaining that "a democracy is more than a form of government; it is primarily a mode of associated living, of conjoint communicated experience" (1916, 87). Areas of common interest form the basis for each person's contribution to the general welfare, and changes in social habit produce freer interaction between social groups. Through education, both of these criteria for a democracy are enhanced and facilitated. As Dewey (1916) phrased it,

> A society which makes provision for participation in its good of all its members on equal terms and which secures flexible readjustment of its institutions through interaction of the different forms of associated life is in so far democratic. Such a society must have a type of education which gives individuals a personal interest in social relationships and control, and the habits of mind which secure social changes without introducing disorder (99).

Calabrese (1990) has put Dewey's philosophical thoughts into more workable form in stating that schools should operate according to principles of an ethical democratic community. Incorporating simple "character education" components into a curriculum in some fashion is not enough. Schools, including curriculum, methodology, student management, organization, and administration, should be places "where justice prevails; where equity is cherished; where integrity is a driving force in all relationships; where full participation is an expectation; where inclusion is a norm; that distribute resources equitably; and that allow members recourse to redress grievances" (12).

Schools as ethical democratic societies must have teachers and administrators who subscribe to basic ethical principles as discussed in Chapter 2 of this textbook and other similar sources. Concepts such as justice, equity, freedom, rights, responsibility, and duty must be shared and must provide the foundation for both general policies and daily operating decisions. This requires much more dialogue among school personnel, students, parents, and the community than is common in most communities.

Differences must be confronted and compromises worked out and agreed upon by all of those "with a stake" in the operations of the school. In this way character will be taught as ethical principles are followed reasonably and consistently. Respect is a guiding standard, even where there is disagreement; respect for every individual's humanity and dignity. Again quoting Dewey (1900), "What the best and wisest parent wants for his own child, that must the community want for all of its children. Any other ideal for our schools is narrow and unlovely; acted upon, it destroys our democracy" (7).

Questions to Guide Ethical Decision Making

As one goes about making decisions that involve ethical considerations, it may be helpful to keep several questions in mind. It won't be possible to go through such a list every time a decision is required, of course, but using appropriate questions to help think about what is important in the situation will help develop appropriate habits and processes.

When a decision or choice is required, the ethical behavior will be that which develops trust, confidence, and integrity in relationships. Ethical behavior will facilitate cooperation and enhance self-respect, avoiding the barriers created by distrust, suspicion, and misunderstanding. Communication will improve and better working relationships will develop, resulting in increased productivity and work satisfaction.

Nash (1996) suggests several kinds of questions to guide our deliberations when decisions involving ethical practice are required. These are discussed in three groups—those that evolve from one's underlying beliefs, those that rely on moral character, and those based on moral principle. Obviously, they are combined and interrelated in actual practice.

Background beliefs answer questions such as "What does it mean to be moral?" and "Is there a spiritual as well as a physical, intellectual, and emotional realm of existence?" One must reach some personally satisfactory conclusions about the source(s) of moral principles, whether an objective morality is possible (or even desirable). If objectivism is considered possible and desirable, how does one avoid the extremes of dogmatism and absolutism? If objectivism is not considered possible, how does one avoid the other extremes of inappropriate relativism and unbridled subjectivism? (40–50).

Moral character refers to "an overall aggregate of moral characteristics that distinguish one person from another." It includes the practice of certain virtues and the avoidance of certain vices, governed by "a complex amalgam of intention, thought, action, disposition, intuition and feeling." It is developed throughout the life of an individual as they interact with a cultural, political, and professional community.

When resolving a moral dilemma, questions such as the following, which are directly or indirectly related to moral character, become part of decision making. What does your "moral instinct" tell you about this case, and what conflicting feelings do you have about it? What would happen if you followed or disregarded your feelings? Are there professional expectations about this case, and should you follow them? (61–67).

Moral principles are developed as a combination of secular or community expectations and personal convictions about virtue and vice. They rest on a moral principle framework that resolves moral dilemmas by logical appeal to accepted rules, guidelines, and theories. Such a framework will probably work best if it includes both deontological and utilitarian approaches, but one or the other will assume a dominant position in each case requiring an ethical decision. A sound decision may thus rely more on a deontological perspective in one case and a utilitarian approach in another, depending on how questions such as the following are answered.

1. Why is this case a moral dilemma?
2. What are the choices in conflict?
3. Who are the morally relevant actors?
4. Where does the action take place?
5. When does the action take place? Is the "when" morally relevant?
6. How is the manner or style of action morally relevant?
7. What are some foreseeable consequences of each decision?
8. What are some foreseeable principles involved in each decision?
9. What are some viable alternatives?
10. What does the code of ethics say? (117).

Nash also suggests a "justification schema" to use in resolving a moral dilemma satisfactorily. It includes the following important questions.

1. What rules do you appeal to in order to justify your decision?
2. What principles do you appeal to in order to justify your decision?
3. What theory do you appeal to in order to justify your decision?
4. What conclusions do you reach regarding your final decision after you compare justifications?
5. What afterthoughts do you have [after] you have made your final decision? (128–145).

Religious Perspectives

Religion has been proposed as a basic ingredient in good education and good educational leadership by more than one person. Referring to a source that most of us would not expect, Parker Palmer states that "Alfred North

Whitehead claimed that all true education is religious education. In the same spirit, all true leadership is religious leadership—for religion has to do with cleansing the human self of the toxins that make our leadership more death-dealing than life-giving" (Greenleaf 1996, xi).

As discussed in Chapter 7, religious beliefs often involve ethical principles. Indeed, there are times when one's religious beliefs may contribute to decision-making dilemmas. For example, choosing a textbook for a biology course will probably involve consideration of its contents relative to the theory of evolution, a theory that some religious groups do not accept. School dress codes and principles of acceptable student behavior often provide dilemmas for school administrators who have strong religious and moral convictions on these subjects. In these kinds of situations, the administrator may be faced with choosing between mores and customs which are generally acceptable to the community and those that are personally more acceptable to him or her (and perhaps some of the staff and constituents). Controversial practices relative to prayer in schools or at school activities, the use of school facilities by religious community or student groups, and acceptable content of library or class literature selections are additional examples of these kinds of dilemmas.

A school administrator who cannot in good conscience accept, and even support, the prevalent ethical and moral positions of a school community has little choice except to move to a community where the prevalent views are personally acceptable. However, in most cases, it is probably possible to tolerate, without accepting, certain practices while working to convince the school community that practices should be more in line with the administrator's beliefs.

Religious ethics requires us to go beyond the maxim "do no harm." Religious beliefs of all kinds have historically proposed that one should not do to others that which they would not want done to them. As discussed by Barclay (1956), this negative form of the Golden Rule was prescribed by one of the best known historical Jewish leaders, Hillel, who taught that "What is hateful to oneself, do to no other; that is the whole Law, and the rest is commentary" (277). Confucius was asked if there is one word that might serve as a general rule of practice, to which he replied "Is not *reciprocity* such a word? What you do not want done to yourself, do not do to others" (278). The Greeks and Romans had similar admonitions. King Nicocles advised his subordinate officials: "Do not do to others the things which make you angry when you experience them at the hands of other people" (278).

Jesus of Nazareth went beyond this negative form to say "Do to others what you would have them do to you" (Matthew 7:12, *The Holy Bible, New International Version* 1973). This puts the principle in a form that is more than a common-sense statement designed to make social discourse possible. "If we could not assume that the conduct and the behavior of other people to us would conform to the accepted standards of civilized life, then life would be intolerable" (Barclay 1956, 279).

The negative form of the rule requires nothing more than not doing certain things. This is not so difficult, and not doing injury to others is typically a legal principle. Inaction would satisfy the negative form of the rule. But when this rule is put in its positive form we must actively do to others what we would have them do to us. Perhaps it is even better to put it that "one should do to others as those others would have done to them," thus following modern psychological principles stressing individual differences. This requires a different attitude and usually much greater purpose, empathy, and effort. Doing no harm to others is much different than doing good to others as they would define good. Again quoting Barclay, "It is quite a simple thing to refrain from hurting and injuring people; it is not so very difficult to respect their principles and their feelings; it is a far harder thing to make it the chosen and deliberate policy of life to go out of our way to be as kind to them as we would wish them to be to us." This requires that we forgive as others wish to be forgiven, to help as others wish to be helped, to praise as others wish to be praised, and to understand as others wish to be understood. One would never seek to avoid doing things, but would always look for things to do in the service of others (280–281). If the world were made up of people who were typically successful in seeking to obey this rule, it would be a different world indeed.

Servant Leadership

Definitions of leadership and the ways leaders are identified are undergoing a radical change in our society. In the past, "strong" leadership was seen to be the imposition of the leader's will upon the led. This was typically done through a system of hierarchical authority, with each person in an organization having one or more bosses, who also had one or more bosses, eventually culminating in the "big boss," who would now probably be called the chief executive officer or CEO. The "big boss" reported to a board of directors or was the "big boss" because he or she was the owner of the business.

In modern societies, it is becoming more and more the case that the most effective leaders are different than those of the past. Various terms are used to describe these leaders, but that of "servant leader" seems to be among the best. This is not so much a type of action or description of leadership behavior as it is an attitude. This attitude may be shown in different behaviors, depending on the personality of the leader and the personality of the organization and the led. Somewhat traditional organizational schemes and leadership behaviors may continue, but at the bottom line of the relationships between leader and followers there is an obvious difference.

The difference between traditional (typically authoritarian) leadership and servant leadership is well stated by Greenleaf (1977).

> The servant-leader *is* servant first . . . It begins with the natural feeling that one wants to serve, to serve *first*. That person is sharply different from one who is *leader* first, perhaps because of the need to assuage an unusual power drive or to acquire material possessions.

The difference [in the servant leader] manifests itself in the care taken by the servant-first to make sure that other people's highest priority needs are being served. The best test and difficult to administer, is: Do those served grow as persons? Do they, while being served, become healthier, wiser, freer, more autonomous, more likely themselves to become servants? (13–14).

The concept of servant leadership is included in most of the major religions. The Christian Bible quotes Jesus as follows. "You know that in the world, rulers lord it over their subjects, and their great men make them feel the weight of authority; but it shall not be so with you. Among you, whoever wants to be great must be your servant, and whoever wants to be first must be the willing slave of all . . ." (Matthew 20:25–28, *The New English Bible*).

If the word "slave" seems too strong or not quite appropriate in it's implications of lack of freedom or involuntary coercion, perhaps we may at least accept some other descriptors of action suggested for the servant-leader. In the first place, the concept requires that one "automatically respond to any problem by listening *first* . . . because listening builds strength in other people. From the prayer of St. Francis, 'Lord, grant that I may not seek so much to be understood as to understand'"(Greenleaf 1977, 17).

Greenleaf (1977), in discussing application of servant leadership concepts in the field of education, first states that, "The ringing phrase from Zechariah, 'Not by might, nor by power, but by my Spirit, says the Lord,'" suggests that in the ancient wisdom there was at least the hope that *might* and *power* might someday be superseded by *spirit* (167). He then expresses specific concern around two fundamental issues for leaders in the field of education:

1. "The assumption that some individuals know what others ought to learn, and are justified in imposing their judgment—backed up by sanctions" (167).
2. "The fact that our whole system of education rests on coercion: first the legal requirement for attending school until age 16–18; then the built-in compulsion to continue academic education by the credentialing that begins with the secondary school diploma and continues through the Ph. D. degree—and beyond" (170).

Greenleaf then proposes that educational leaders "add something that is voluntary, something that raises the human spirit. See if the urge to venture further does not overtake you" (172). This in pursuit of a goal "to prepare students to serve and be served by the present society" (190).

McGee (1986) provides some additional help in understanding the attitude and behavior of the effective servant leader. He points out that servant leaders are also willing to sacrifice self in the interests of others. They are willing to admit errors instead of trying to place the blame on others. They are willing to put others in a position to receive credit, even when most credit might rightfully belong to the leader.

Servant leaders are willing and able to empathize, to understand *and* jointly feel with others. Again, listening, indicating understanding, and giving suggestions, instead of always giving orders or instructions, becomes important in helping the leader to sense the feelings of others and allow them to develop their own ways of dealing with their feelings and figuring out how to solve various problems. This ability, of course, includes understanding the strengths and weaknesses of others in the group and providing for the best adjustments in the situation or the organization to accommodate those strengths and weaknesses.

One must not get the idea, however, that the servant leader just "goes with the flow," failing to guide when guidance is necessary. The servant leader must also be able to see above the crowd. Both dangers and opportunities must be recognized, ultimate purposes followed, and clear direction given to the group in a way that shows self-confidence but not self-centeredness.

Building on self-sacrifice and empathy, the servant leader is also able and willing to be tolerant—tolerant of others' differences and even their mistakes. They, in turn, will be more tolerant of the leader's mistakes and weaknesses.

One outcome of following most religious traditions would be more acceptance of and success in achieving servant leadership. As discussed above, this concept takes our usual understanding of the Golden Rule and further suggests that we should treat others as they would like to be treated. Perhaps they would like to be treated just as we would like to be treated in similar circumstances, but human relations experts now propose that, because people have different likes and dislikes, treating others as we would like to be treated may not satisfy the desires of those "others." They may want to be treated differently in similar circumstances than we personally would prefer.

Stephen Covey's "seven habits" and what is implied in their application include most of those attributes and actions advocated by many who have studied and written about effective leadership. They are the foundation for most current writing on how to become a good leader, and they will not be repeated or reviewed here. However, the "habits" that are included in a "paradigm of interdependence" are particularly appropriate to this discussion of how ethical principles should be incorporated into effective leadership behavior.

The "Win/Win" part of Covey's paradigm stresses the importance of cooperation, emphasizing that to motivate people to cooperate requires a situation in which there is not just one or a few winners. It must be possible for all of the group in which cooperation is desired to become "winners" in their own eyes. There must be a common goal, the achievement of which results in individually perceived advantage. There are no losers.

> Win/Win is a frame of mind and heart that constantly seeks mutual benefit in all human interactions. Win/Win means that agreements or solutions are mutually beneficial, mutually satisfying. With a Win/Win solution, all parties feel good about the decision and feel committed to the action plan (207).

Drawing on the concept expressed by St. Francis mentioned above, (to understand rather than to be understood), Covey also endorses the importance of "empathic listening." We typically are most concerned that others understand our viewpoint and preferences, when the concept of interdependence requires a different emphasis. Instead of listening "with the intent to understand [we] listen with the intent to reply" (239). Empathic listening will allow one to "diagnose before prescribing," and be more likely to lead to mutually acceptable decisions and courses of action. The more selfish goal of being understood (and having personal goals accepted) is then more likely to be achieved.

According to Covey, and other writers who follow a similar line of thought, following the concepts expressed above may lead to "creative cooperation" and a **synergy** of thought and action. Synergy is described as the "highest activity in all life—the true test and manifestation of all of the other habits put together." Through synergy new alternatives may be created as the power of cooperation and mutual effort catalyze and unify the creativity and energy of those involved. Synergy is thus defined as when the whole actually becomes greater than the sum of its parts (262–263).

In the last section of his book, Covey quotes Ezra Taft Benson to illustrate the notion that the most productive human growth occurs from the "inside-out," a process required to achieve best the seven habits. Expressed from a particular religious perspective, the principle illustrated seems applicable from other religious and non-religious views, as well.

> The Lord works from the inside out. The world works from the outside in. The world would take people out of the slums. Christ takes the slums out of people, and then they take themselves out of the slums. The world would mold men by changing their environment. Christ changes men, who then change their environment. The world would shape human behavior, but Christ can change human nature (309).

Aspiration Ethics

It may be noted from our earlier consideration of deontological, teleological, and virtue ethics that there is movement from what might be termed a minimalist ethic to one that reaches for greater and greater heights of human moral life and expectations. As discussed by Pojman (2002), it is somewhat humbling to note that Socrates, Plato, and Aristotle must be given credit for long ago developing most of what is called the ethics of aspiration and which we have discussed under the label "virtue ethics" (255–259). Going beyond the dictum "do no harm" or other minimal standards for ethical conduct which rely on a core of necessary rules to guide human conduct, aspiration ethics calls on us to continually reach for greater heights of moral understanding and ethical conduct. Benefit to others (beneficence) is required, rather than simply avoiding harm to others (non-maleficence).

At what may be considered a lower level of moral development, traditional rule-based ethics seeks to maintain a society that is primarily concerned with maintaining basic rights, allowing people to live their lives unhindered by other humans, government or other organizational controls. It appeals to minimal common sense and can be more easily universalized, although there are obvious difficulties in the more absolutist positions.

Moving "along the continuum" of moral thinking, teleology requires sometimes difficult and challenging efforts to consider the consequences of actions, making moral decisions more through reason and judgment. Except for those who take a strong utilitarian position, however, there is still little motivation to take positive steps to better the human condition. The emphasis continues to be on avoiding harm or unnecessary restriction on the freedom of others.

Classical virtue ethics stresses the pervasive nature of ethics in human life, not allowing for compartmentalizing life into activities requiring high levels of ethical conduct and those allowing less restriction imposed by ethical standards. "Business is business" excuses are not accepted to justify lower standards of ethics than would be expected in other settings. One is expected to practice on Monday what is preached on Sunday.

An ethics of aspiration also calls for a continual and life-long climb to advance both the ability *for* and the accomplishment *of* ethical living. As stated by Pojman (2002), we may not all be expected to become either heroes or saints, but aspiration ethics challenges us all to grow toward heroic and saintly levels of action in our daily lives. What does this mean in concrete terms? It means that good deeds are accomplished in spite of fear or self-interest (heroic action) and acts for good prevail regardless of our inclinations toward personal desire or self-interest (saintly action). Our duty is to grow in both heroic and saintly terms as a moral person, both in our willingness and our ability to accept moral responsibility and pursue related ethical actions (256–257). A set of descriptors such as that developed by Kohlberg may serve as a guide and provide standards for our moral development, but only individual determination and daily reflection can assure success in reaching higher levels of moral living.

Ethical Bricolage

We often experience difficulty in accommodating contrasting and sometimes competing concepts to ethical action. Trying to arrive at some golden mean of philosophical standard and ethical decision making while considering the differing views of deontology, teleology, or virtue ethics may become daunting, to say the least. In addition, the daily and often urgent demands of educational administration don't readily accommodate the time, thought, or understanding that seems necessary. So the tendency is to say "that's too theoretical" and rely excessively on tradition, custom, or personal inclination—to "fly by the seat of our pants," to put it in the vernacular.

Is there a way to be both thoughtful and practical, to get help from theory and historical thought without sacrificing efficiency? Perhaps so, by applying the concept of "bricolage" to ethics and ethical decision making. The Oxford English Dictionary (1993) defines *bricolage* as the "construction or creation from whatever is immediately available for use; an assemblage of haphazard or incongruous elements."

Applied to the study of ethics and ethical practice, *bricolage* (according to Schwehn 1993) means "the creative synthesis of vocabularies and practices borrowed from different, sometimes competing, moral and religious traditions into an ethical discourse that is flexible enough to meet emergencies and surprises yet steady, humane, and principled enough to provide for human flourishing." How one constructs such a bricolage probably "becomes much more a matter of feelings, attitudes, inclinations, and character than . . . some thinly described rational deliberation, even presumably a deliberation informed by an eclectic set of beliefs" (55). Nash (1996) supports this statement in arguing that "in the spirit of moral bricolage, . . . ethical decisions are shaped by the interrelationship of several elements: personal philosophies, metaphysical beliefs, the virtues, communities, narratives, rules, principles, circumstances, consequences, feelings, intuitions, codes of ethics, training, and workplace norms" (147).

Ethical bricolage also seems to include concepts discussed in Chapter 7 as *situation ethics*. This approach suggests that one should make use of ethical maxims and community mores, but as illuminators rather than unbending legalisms. One must sometimes compromise ethical rules or codes in a particular situation if that is required to fulfill the greater value of "brotherly love." Reason should be consulted to balance the demands of both natural law and divine law if the highest standards of love seem better served by doing so.

According to situation ethics, every moral decision involves viewing the total context and consideration of the ends, the means, the motives, and the probable effects of any action, as well as appropriate rules, maxims, codes, or moral principles. Ethics, according to this view, aims at a contextual appropriateness—not so much the "good" or the "right" as the "fitting." Circumstances may therefore alter rules and principles.

Core Values (Principle Ethics)

Although one may accept the suggestion that "aspiration ethics" and "ethical bricolage" have some use in ethical decision making, it is still necessary to have some basic foundation upon which to lay these accessories to action. Personal tendencies, brought on by a lifetime of experiences, make it impossible to be entirely objective and accurate in making ethical decisions. In the words of former U.S. President Jimmy Carter (1998), "It is difficult for any of us to assess our own habits and actions objectively. Without a set of guidelines, it is not possible to acknowledge and correct the mistakes, beliefs and habits that tend to become a way of life" (46).

A personal set of principles to guide one's actions will be just that—personal, but it should be subject to principles of caring and justice and continuously subjected to review and critique. It will include, but probably not be limited to the following:

1. Philosophical and historical thought
2. Current moral and ethical guidelines
3. Best professional practice
4. Principles of democracy and justice
5. Personal convictions

It must be carefully noted once again, however, that if one accepts the notion that objectivity is not the last word in ethics, then all principles and convictions remain open to review, question, and revision.

Behind principle ethics lies a concept expressed by some as one's "vocation" or "calling." This concept differentiates between one's vocation and one's career or occupation. Vocation is seen as that which guides the work or other activities of life. It reflects the core of our being and our personhood.

As explained by Palmer (2000), living according to our "vocation" means living according to what the humanist tradition calls identity and integrity. It "does not mean a goal that I pursue. It means a calling that I hear" (4). A vocation is a specific call to love one's neighbor through the duties that come to us as we live our lives, utilizing personal talents and gifts in our work, our families, and all other social relationships. Whatever the situation and circumstances, one is to [demonstrate]. . . "love, joy, peace, patience, kindness, goodness, faithfulness, gentleness, and self-control" (Hardy 1990, 81).

For educational administrators, the concept of vocation described above shows itself in everyday decisions and actions. Leadership becomes something that evolves from the concept of community. Again quoting Palmer, "if it is true that we are made for community, then leadership is everyone's vocation . . . When we live in the close-knit ecosystem called community, everyone follows and everyone leads." The power for authentic leadership "is found not in external arrangements but in the human heart" (75–76). The "human heart" in this context is not an individual concept, it is collective. As leaders, "we fulfill our vocation in partnership with others" and "learn with others." (Smith 1999, 163, 172).

Concluding Reflections

The idea for this book began several years ago as this author saw the need for a workable process of ethical decision making for educational leaders. A review of the literature on effective leadership, particularly leadership in the field of education, seemed to indicate that much of what was effective leadership was ethical in nature. Both long-range and everyday decisions required of educational leaders almost always have ethical overtones, but the need for training in this aspect of educational leadership seemed to be neglected in both the initial preparation and the ongoing professional development of educational leaders.

So now we come to the point of trying to reach some conclusions and describe a process for educational leaders to follow as they attempt to act in professional and ethical ways to solve the dilemmas and problems encountered in educational institutions. But the task of describing such a process seems to become more and more difficult as we study the wisdom of past and present leaders, researchers, and thinkers about the topic. Life, and particularly life in educational settings, is too complicated to allow acceptance of a single process to follow in decision making. Human beings don't always fit the mold that a single process of decision making would require.

So how to conclude this study of ethics and ethical decision making? If we can't settle on one acceptable process to learn and apply, what can be done to help us become more ethical, and thereby more effective, leaders?

First it must be recognized that one never finishes the study of ethics and ethical decision making. It is a life-long process, guided by the intent to progressively become a more ethical person and a better leader. It becomes ever more apparent that "the more we know, the more we know we don't know."

Perhaps the best we can do is to learn as much as possible about the options available, their uses, advantages, disadvantages, and misuses, and then develop a process to fit the occasion. Similarities may be evident in the varying processes used in different situations, but there will be room for innovation and adaptation. Following this approach, the remainder of this book will review some of the more important concepts already studied and how they may be used and combined. Some additional related ideas will also be addressed as they may appear helpful to the serious student of ethical and effective educational leadership. This won't reach the end of our study, but it will reach the end of this book and lead us into a life-long process of reflective practice.

Seeing Things Whole.   A prerequisite to good decision making in any leadership context, and particularly so when ethical considerations are involved, has to do with "seeing the big picture," or, as Greenleaf (1977) puts it, "seeing things whole." The basic requirement is that we know where we are, where we have been (or the foundations of our journey), and where we are going—all in a context as large and complete as we can construct and understand. To thus "see things whole" refers to one's total perception of a situation and understanding the relationships and interactions taking place. Again, it is a case of "the whole being bigger than the sum of its parts," so perception, analysis, and synthesis all become part of "getting the big picture."

"Seeing things whole" as an educational administrator means, among other things, that all of the students and staff an administrator is supposed to be leading are seen as individuals with personal needs and dreams. At the same time, they are seen as part of an educational system, a community, and other social and economic systems that have their own sets of needs and aspirations.

Good leadership and good ethical practice thus becomes much more than the consistent application of rules and regulations or the efficient accomplishment of a particular task. "Johnny" is seen to be more than a discipline problem, for example, with specific behaviors to be controlled. He is seen in a context of personal and social realities, all of which must be dealt with to adequately deal with Johnny's "bad" behavior.

"Seeing things whole" requires that one who is called on to make a decision with ethical considerations must go beyond applying rules and regulations. Decisions must be made and actions taken that are consistent with a system of ethics and morals which includes intent and consequences as well as duties and rules. This both *draws on* and *contributes to* what Greenleaf (1996) describes as the "human spirit."

> I have noted that seeing things whole and spirit are interacting qualities, each nourishing the other. Confidence to act on anything in the world of affairs is bolstered by the assurance that one sees the situation whole. Willingness to follow the leadership of another rests somewhat on the belief that the other person sees things whole and is likely to be dependable. The quality of seeing things whole is to me an element of faith as trust—trust in oneself, trust in others, and trust in a doctrinal position (134).

The "Borromean knot" of Olympic games fame, as suggested by Haynes (1998), illustrates the need to see the big picture and recognize the importance of each part of an ethical decision-making plan. When any one of the rings is cut, the entire interlocking system falls apart, illustrating the fact that each part of the whole is equally important—consistency (rules and guidelines), consequences, and care. Jointly they constitute a sound base for ethical decision making. Leaving out one of these essentials will typically lead to less than satisfactory results.

"Seeing things whole" also allows us to deal better with the ambiguities that inevitably accompany problems and other situations requiring administrative and ethical decisions. Educators, and probably most people in general, want to avoid ambiguity. We tend to be uncomfortable with doubt and uncertainty, particularly those situations that may be understood in two or more different ways. It is tempting to place undue trust in quantified data such as test scores and property values, failing in these and others ways to distinguish between practicality, efficiency, economy, productivity, and morality. "For those who accept this way of thinking ambiguous, uncertain, nonmeasurable dimensions of schools often are dismissed or ignored" (Beck 1994, 92–93).

But ambiguity cannot be avoided in education or life in general. We cannot be guilty of tendencies described by Winston Churchill, who "is reported to have once observed that the French have a way of making things much clearer than God ever intended them to be" (Rohr 1989, 2). Uncertainties must be dealt with, such as:

1. Situations where competitive and institutional pressures undermine one's best intentions.
2. Times when we are not sure if our actions or those of others are unethical.
3. Times when we feel a genuine obligation to fulfill the needs of others but are not sure about how to best do it.
4. Situations where our personal preferences or well-being seem to conflict with those of others.
5. Difficulties in pleasing different constituencies (Childs 1995, 124).

Seeing things whole may be facilitated by thinking of those Russian dolls that we bring out with our Christmas decorations—a smaller doll nestled inside a larger doll nestled inside yet a larger doll. At the core are the standards, rules, and maxims embodied in deontology. The next doll exemplifies concern for consequences and basic purposes. A third doll may represent the ethic of care and situation ethics. All fit closely to each other and constitute the whole.

The last point we will consider relative to seeing things whole relates to the concept of valuation, as related to values. As explained by Willower and Licata (1997), "moral choice in administration is really a matter of *valuation,* a term we use to refer to the process of choosing from and implementing conceptions of the desirable with an awareness of and sensitivity to their potential consequences for a variety of individuals and groups, as well as the multiplicity of values typically affected by implementation." Emphasizing valuation, rather than values alone, adds meaning to habits, rituals, and rules that tend to separate them from real life. Reflective practice shows the common faults of packaged answers and slogan-like quick fixes, as a problem is clearly understood, alternative courses of action considered, and results of the action chosen tested as thoroughly and objectively as possible (26–27).

Choosing a Model

Flexibility and eclecticism are fine up to a point, but one must eventually settle on a course of action when confronted with dilemmas and other situations requiring administrative decisions. Some model or process for use in doing so would seem to be helpful, as envisioned at the beginning of this book. Many theories, ideas, and approaches have been discussed. Which ones seem most appropriate to some kind of model? The limb is long and fragile, but it is vital to find some answers to the many questions that have been considered and among the even more numerous answers proposed.

A process to achieve a goal, or a series of actions to take, is often proposed in a sequential pattern. Do this first, then this, then something else. It seems, however, that if one is trying to "see things whole," as proposed above, then a series of actions may take different forms in different situations. There may be a sequence that is most common, but it may not always be best. The following suggestions are made, therefore, not as a series of thoughts or actions, but as a group to be considered and used in the sequence or combination most appropriate in each case.

Philosophical and Ethical Theory. The three major theories discussed in this book have been labeled deontology, teleology, and virtue ethics. Rather than rely on one or the other as a theory to guide actions, perhaps the following approach would be best, progressing in spiral fashion with possible cutbacks and reconsiderations.

1. Use deontology to guide thinking relative to what is more clearly right and wrong. A set of rules or maxims, even a code of ethics, would seem to be most useful if the question at hand is somewhat black and white, without the conflicting and confusing side issues that "muddy the water" and create a legitimate dilemma. A word of caution, however—a set of rules may in itself make something appear to be more "black and white" than it really is, resulting in ignoring or neglecting legitimate moral issues that should not be ignored. Justice and basic human rights may not be neglected in the interests of legal or institutional interests, mores, or historical precedent.

2. Use teleology to guide decisions when what is right or wrong is not obvious and when a "higher" principle must be favored in cases in which two or more rules or principles call for different actions. Consider the consequences of action in terms of what will produce the most good and do the least harm.

3. Use virtue ethics to focus on the well being of others, to develop habits and attributes of a "good person." Care for others (the Golden Rule with appropriate variations to insure fair and loving treatment) thus becomes the ultimate guide to ethical decision making. The specific situation and varying circumstances must be carefully considered and decisions adjusted accordingly.

Elements of a Process. Although they may not always proceed in the same sequence in different situations, there are some essential elements that should be included in efforts to make ethical decisions and act on them. Using moral creativity, give attention to the following.

1. Get the facts. The relevant and important facts will vary with the case, but the following questions are typical of those that will probably need attention. Is there a moral issue—something obviously wrong personally, interpersonally or socially? What individuals and groups have an important stake in the outcome? What is at stake for each and do some have a greater stake because they have a special need or because we have special obligations to them? Besides those directly involved, are there others with a legitimate and important interest? What are the roles involved, including

the codes, or value subsystems, that guide their enactment? Identifying and clarifying the relevant facts of the case may resolve a dilemma by developing mutual understanding of concerns and positions among those involved if there is adequate communication among the stakeholders

2. Identify the ethical issues. They may usually be stated in terms of conflicting interests or benefits, such as the good of the individual versus the good of a group, short-term versus long-term benefits, justice and fairness, and other ethical principles discussed earlier.

3. Identify the ethical and moral principles from deontology, teleology, and value ethics that are related to the issues of the case. Decide if some principles should be weighted more heavily or given precedence over others.

4. Determine criteria for a good resolution of the problem or dilemma, based on identified moral principles to be considered. Develop some descriptors of action that would be consistent with important principles, perhaps making use of one or more codes of ethics.

5. Develop several viable alternative solutions. Avoid the temptation to rely on the most common or most readily available possibilities and try to be "creative" without using too much time and energy in attempting to be exhaustive.

6. Weigh the consequences of the most likely alternative solutions. Without getting caught up in a "paralysis of analysis," with the time and resources available, make the best projections possible about both short-term and long-term outcomes. How would your role and the roles of others be affected? Which options best respect the rights and dignity of all concerned? Will the common good be best achieved and those virtues or character traits we value as individuals, professionals and members of society deepened and developed?

7. Apply relevant principles and criteria to the solutions being considered and their probable consequences. Does there seem to be a good fit?

8. Consider how you would feel about the most likely solutions. Anticipate how you would feel about *yourself* if you adopted each of the most likely actions being considered. How would you justify each alternative to the most obvious stakeholders, to someone you respect, and to a broad public?

9. Make a decision. Realizing that there are no easy or painless decisions to difficult problems or dilemmas.

10. Reflect on the decision later. How did it work out for all concerned? If you were doing it again, would you do anything differently? Why? Is additional or supplemental action called for?

Measures of Success.   We all want to feel successful in doing what we think is important, but how may we best measure success as educational leaders? Few would argue the notion that a good leader must lead by example, for as the old saying goes, "actions speak louder than words." It then follows that if we would like to have some part in developing a better, more ethical organization and society, then we must try to see that what we do as a leader sets the ethical tone and helps create the moral environment of the organization. Codes of conduct and related policies and procedures are necessary in developing a moral and ethical climate in an organization, but it is the leader's personal conduct that is most influential. Greenleaf (1996) emphasizes the importance of ethical leadership by example in this statement. "It is reported that a king once asked Confucius what to do about thievery among his subjects. The answer was, 'if you sir, were not covetous, they would not steal—even if you urged them to do it'" (311).

Are there some ways that one may judge success as an ethical leader? No one will become perfect, of course, but, without becoming overly ambitious in our desire to be ethical, are there some signs that might be encouraging and supporting? Perhaps some signs of growth is the best we can hope for. As stated by Dewey (1920),

> Not perfection as a final goal, but the ever-enduring process of perfecting, maturing, refining, is the aim in living . . . The bad man is the man who, no matter how good he has been, is beginning to deteriorate, to grow less good. The good man is the man who, no matter how morally unworthy he *has* been, is moving to become better. Such a conception makes one severe in judging himself and humane in judging others (176–177).

The following questions (and others you may apply to individual concerns and situations) may be helpful as you seek to assess success in ethical educational leadership and set goals for improvement.

1. What school administrator practices violate the principle of viewing the school as a democratic community? What might school administrators do to more fully implement the principle of viewing the school as a democratic community?
2. What background beliefs influence your thinking when confronted with a difficult decision that involves ethical considerations? Upon what fundamental ethical principles do you base difficult decisions that have ethical implications?
3. Are you able to overcome biases and preconceived ideas in assessing difficult situations and arriving at decisions?
4. What are some dangers relative to allowing religious beliefs to influence your thinking as a school administrator? What should you do when your religious beliefs conflict with commonly accepted practices in a school district? Think about some specific examples of how this might occur.
5. Do you believe in servant leadership? If so, give some examples of how it might be applied by school administrators.
6. Even if you believe in servant leadership, do you think there are situations in which it is not practical or advisable? If so, give some examples.

7. Do you believe that an ethics of aspiration is a viable concept? What difficulties would exist in its implementation as a school administrator?

8. What problems or dangers do you see in accepting and implementing the concept of ethical bricolage as a school administrator? What value do you see in doing so?

9. What makes it difficult sometimes for school administrators to "see things whole"?

10. What model or combination of models discussed in this book do you believe will work best for you to follow as a school administrator when called upon to make difficult decisions involving ethical considerations?

11. Are you treating others as you would want to be treated, or perhaps more importantly, as *they* want to be treated?

12. How will you judge whether or not you are successful as an ethical leader?

Only the individual can measure personal growth in ethical matters, because no one else can know another person's intimate purposes, struggles, failures, and successes. As we each undertake this personal and ongoing analysis and judgment, making use of all we can muster from the wisest of the past and present, our greatest encouragement will be to know that "the joy is in the journey."

Case Studies

Choosing Leaders

Drew is principal of a large suburban high school and encounters a "right versus right" dilemma. The chair of the twelve-teacher science department is retiring and must recommend a replacement. Two of the current members of the department have applied for the position, which carries a $10,000 pay stipend and one-half teaching load. The previous department chair was well-liked and effective in bringing the department to a high level of competence and success with student achievement.

One of the teachers who has applied for the department chair position is a woman with about fifteen years teaching experience, all in the same school. Roxanne is exceptionally creative and talented in presenting material to students and in developing unique and interesting ways to organize the lessons and student assignments. She also serves as cheerleader sponsor, is very involved with parents and various community activities, and is exceptionally popular with both students and parents. Last year she was recognized as "teacher of the year" at the school.

Calvin, the other applicant, has taught for about twenty years in the school. Calvin is also known as a very good teacher, although his methods are traditional, and students sometimes comment that his classes are not particularly exciting. They do, however, usually reach high levels of achievement. He is exceptionally well-organized and well-prepared for classes, normally arriving at the school early and leaving late preparing for class, grading papers, and taking care of other responsibilities. Calvin's "extra duty" responsibilities have included providing leadership in preparing curriculum guides, choosing textbooks, and other important organizational work of the department and the school. Without exception, these duties are carried out willingly and efficiently. Several of his students have gone on to careers in science and medicine and given him credit for preparing them well for their careers.

Calvin is respected by his colleagues, although he has no close friends among the faculty. This respect is carried over to students and parents. He is active in his church, but not in other community organizations.

On the other hand, Roxanne isn't known for either efficiency or punctuality. Her organizational style can best be described an "unique," although she has assured Drew that she can certainly take care of organizational matters and learn to be more prompt in completing paper work and other administrative chores. She is more concerned about student attitudes than standardized test scores, although her students seem to achieve satisfactorily on the state mandated tests.

Informal conversations with the members of the department and Drew's gut feeling indicate that a slight majority of the teachers in the department and the school as a whole believe Calvin should be the new department chair. They believe that he would be the better administrator and more effective in facilitating the work of teachers and taking care of organizational matters. The feeling among the other teachers is strongly in favor of Roxanne, because of her outgoing leadership qualities, innovation, and general popularity with students and parents.

Drew knows that he himself is not considered particularly innovative or progressive in his leadership and there has been some criticism in the community about the lack of females in leadership positions in the school and the school district. Another matter of some concern to Drew is the fact that Calvin's wife works for one of the school board members.

Questions to Consider

1. How would you rank criteria for selection of a high school science department chair?
2. What process should be followed to develop a recommendation to the superintendent and board of education?
3. How important is the matter of male-female balance in school and school leadership personnel?
4. How important is the matter of seniority in this situation?
5. How much attention should be given to the "political" aspects of this case?
6. What are likely to be the short-term and long-term consequences of naming one or the other of the candidates to the department chair position?

A Matter of Priorities

Oil Town has a long history of success in school athletics, particularly football. Arnold, the superintendent of schools, is faced with a difficult decision. Three years ago, the previous football coach retired after a long history of success. In fact, he was somewhat of a legend in the community and the state. He still lives in the community and regularly has coffee with town leaders, especially members of the athletic booster club.

When the previous coach retired, his long-time assistant and defensive coordinator, Alex, was named head coach. Alex was an excellent assistant coach in every way. His technical coaching skills are superb and recognized across the state, as proven by his regular invitations to make presentations at coaching clinics. He is an outstanding role model for students. His character and moral standards have never been questioned in the community. In addition, Alex is very active in various community activities and the Fellowship of Christian Athletes. Arnold is particularly impressed with Alex's record of success in promoting academic achievement among the football players; several have gone on to college success as both players and students.

There is still a problem. The football team has not reached the district finals in the last three years. Their record of wins only slightly exceeds their record of losses, and "the natives are getting restless." Arnold received in today's mail a letter signed by over a hundred community members, including a majority of the board of education, expressing extreme disappointment with the record of the football team since Alex became head football coach. The letter recommends that the current offensive coordinator, "Flash" Gorden, be made head coach. The offensive coordinator was brought in by Alex. He is very energetic, dedicated, and known by the "Monday morning quarterbacks" as an innovative and demanding coach. The letter expresses the belief that Alex has been limiting Flash's effectiveness by being too conservative and traditional in his style of play and "game night" decisions. It recommends (more accurately, demands) that Alex be fired and the offensive coordinator named head coach. Similar sentiment has been expressed in recent sports pages of the local newspaper and several letters to the editor.

Arnold thinks highly of Alex as a person, as an influence in the community, and as a role model for students. They are also good friends and play golf together. On the other hand, he has received what he believes to be valid information over a period of time that Flash's personal and professional ethics, his behavior as a role model for students, and his priorities relative to student academic achievement are quite different than those of Alex.

Questions to Consider

1. What educational priorities should govern decisions about school athletics?
2. What aspects of school and community relations should influence decisions about school athletics?

3. What procedures should be followed relative to appointment and reappointment of athletic coaches? Should they be different from those for classroom teachers or school administrators?
4. Rank priorities for a head athletic coach.
5. What immediate actions should the superintendent take in this situation?
6. How should a decision be made about replacing a head coach?
7. What might be done to "mend political fences" in this case?
8. Should the superintendent become "good friends" with the head football coach? or any school employee?

Activities and Discussion Questions

1. Conduct short interviews with teachers and students to inquire whether they consider their school "a democratic community."

2. Which of your background beliefs are strongest in guiding your ethical decisions?

3. Rank order the ten most important core values of your personal belief system.

4. Which of your core values sometimes conflict in ethical decision making?

5. When your core values conflict, what do you do?

6. How might the concept of vocation as explained by Palmer and others impact your life priorities and ethics?

7. Interview one or more practicing school administrators and get their reaction to the ten process elements suggested in this chapter for use in making ethical decisions.

8. Give some examples of when one or more senior administrators were not given accurate or adequate information. Why did this occur?

9. Discuss the concept of servant leadership with at least one teacher and one administrator. How do their views of this concept differ? How are they similar?

10. How do religious beliefs impact ethical decision making?

11. Develop a personal set of principles and process elements for ethical decision making.

12. Write a concluding paragraph for this textbook.

References

Barclay, W. (1956). *The gospel of Matthew, vol. 1*. Philadelphia: The Westminster Press.
Beck, L. G. and Murphy, J. (1994). *Ethics in educational leadership programs: An expanding role*. Thousand Oaks, CA: Corwin Press.
Calabrese, R. L. (1990.) The school as an ethical and democratic community. *NASSP Bulletin*, 74, 10–15.
Carter, J. (1998). *Living faith*. New York: Random House.

Childs, J. M., Jr. (1995). *Ethics in business: Faith at work.* Minneapolis: Fortress Press

Covey, S. R. (1989). *The seven habits of highly effective people.* New York: Simon & Schuster.

Dewey, J. (1900). *The school and society.* Chicago: The University of Chicago Press.

Dewey, J. (1916). *Democracy and education.* New York: Macmillan.

Dewey, J. (1920). *Reconstruction in philosophy.* New York: Holt.

The encyclopedia Americana, International edition, vol. 8. (1986). Danbury, CT: Grolier.

Greenleaf, R. K. (1977). *Servant Leadership.* New York: Paulist Press.

Greenleaf, R. K. (1996). *Seeker and servant: Reflections on religious leadership.* Fraker, A. T. and L. C. Spears, eds. San Francisco: Jossey-Bass.

Hardy, L. (1990). *The fabric of this world.* Grand Rapids, MI: William B. Eerdmans Publishing.

Haynes, F. (1998). *The ethical school.* New York and London: Routledge.

The Holy Bible, New International Version. International Bible Society, 1973.

Kohlberg, L. (1984). The psychology of moral development. *Essays on moral development, vol. 2.* San Francisco: Harper & Row.

McGee, D. B. (1986). The ethics of leadership. Paper presented at the meeting of the National Congress on Leadership, Gatlinburg, TN.

Nash, R. J. (1996) *Real world ethics.* New York: Teachers College Press.

The New English Bible, (1970). New York: Oxford University Press.

Palmer, J. (2000). *Let your life speak.* San Francisco: Jossey-Bass.

Pojman, L. P. (2002). *Ethics: Discovering right and wrong,* 4th ed. Belmont, CA: Wadsworth.

Random House Webster's college dictionary. (1992). New York: Random House.

Rohr, J. A. (1989). *Ethics for bureaucrats,* 2nd ed. New York: Marcel Dekker, Inc.

Schwehn, M. R. (1993). *Exiles from Eden.* New York: Oxford University Press.

Smith, G. T. (1999). *Courage and calling.* Downers Grove, IL: InterVarsity Press.

Willower, D. J., and Licata, J. W. (1997). *Values and valuation in the practice of educational administration.* Thousand Oaks, CA: Corwin Press.

Index